I0449120

A Village
Waits For You

A VILLAGE
WAITS FOR YOU

RAY CRYER

authorHOUSE®

AuthorHouse™
1663 Liberty Drive
Bloomington, IN 47403
www.authorhouse.com
Phone: 1-800-839-8640

© 2010 Ray Cryer. All rights reserved.

No part of this book may be reproduced, stored in a retrieval system, or transmitted by any means without the written permission of the author.

First published by AuthorHouse   2/2/2010

ISBN: 978-1-4490-7257-5 (e)
ISBN: 978-1-4490-7256-8 (sc)
ISBN: 978-1-4490-7255-1 (hc)

Library of Congress Control Number: 2010900186

Printed in the United States of America
Bloomington, Indiana

This book is printed on acid-free paper.

INTRODUCTION

The story which follows is not the story of a super, extraordinary man doing expected, grand feats. Rather, it is the story of a very ordinary person doing something rather spectacular that almost anyone could duplicate. I am neither rich, nor well connected, an intellectual, nor a true holy man. Nor was I an early bloomer that focused on a goal in my teens and through force of will, made it come into fruition. I was not a superb athlete and will never make the Guinness Book of Records or the national news. Outside of having the good fortune to have had some extensive travels, Ray Cryer can be found on every street in America. Yet, because I am so very ordinary, I aspire to hold out hope to others seeking to escape the maelstrom of conformity. My hope is that they may lose themselves in some cause larger than self. For I believe it is important that every man and woman become the hero of his or her own life story. This is not the only way to do it, but it is certainly one way. You don't have to search your closet for a super hero's costume – you are already in it. Deeds make it fit.

In writing this book, rarely has an author's expectations for success been so low. In the end it may be as much of an advertisement as a book, rather like an Uncle Sam poster saying "I want you". No matter how accomplished an author I could become, the material ropes me into a narrow corral. It is too serious to be amusing, yet not poignant enough to bring tears to the eyes. And even if I could make the reader tearful, I would be working at cross-purposes to myself to do so. It would be rather like me volunteering to work at an animal shelter. I cannot because it would break my heart and immobilize me. With such sadness afoot, I am better off merely contributing money and leaving the work to my betters.

If I am able to encourage one other person to pick a village and make a beginning, then my work is well repaid. And, not to believe they must be part of a team, subject to someone else's orders, fulfilling someone else's plan.

It is important that people cast away all unrealistic fears. Among those is the fantasy that upon arrival in the village the people will fall on you taking your life and money. I have never found pressure beyond that of a person in rags hoping, but not really expecting, that I would help. And your ethnicity means nothing to them. In Haiti for example, I found not the barest shred of evidence that those of African descent would want to harm a Caucasian because of historical grievances real or imagined.

Further, it doesn't critically matter whether the self-proclaimed helper has hands on skill or not. Learned skills are however, always an asset, and the need for them may pop up at the most unexpected times. I would always recommend pre-project study on gardening and topics dealing with water, plus whatever could be learned about the culture into which the helper is going. But these are not essential. What is essential is to listen, have respect for the people you are among, and have the ability to know a good idea when you hear one, with the personal pluck to make a decision. And while money is certainly an asset, and I take along as much of that root of evil as I can, it is surprising how much can be done with so little. The dollar stretches much further in a village than in America. Of all you can pack or carry with you however, the most essential element, in my experience, is to stick close to God. He has a way of making unlikely things work out for those who do. He is subtle – as subtle as an anonymous giver, yet I spot Him. I see His fingerprints on all that which is good. And, I certainly cannot say that He helps only helpers that are believers, because there are far more people involved in the equation than just the helper. There are hundreds of villagers, many of whom have been praying long and hard. Your mere presence among them, with even meager resources, will be like wind in the sail of a boat that has been in the doldrums.

CHAPTER 1

The Milwaukee Journal labeled me a humanist crusader, The Houston Post referred to me as a "god", and the Yucatan Dario proclaimed me in words I have yet to translate. The Dallas Morning News announced the establishment of "The Cryer Foundation," and described "A Texan's Do-It Yourself Foreign Aid." My local newspaper, the Cherokeean Herald, described me as a "one-man Peace Corps" and later titled their front-page with "When a Village isn't enough, send the Town's Cryer." Both a tropical road and a village were named after my wife. It would all have been enough to inflate my ego like a weather balloon if I had not learned that today's news coats the bottom of a birdcage before week's end.

Before all that, my life was chiefly like time spent in a crowded barbershop on a Saturday morning. Like the village well, we congregated there to avoid work while still seeming to take care of business. Too, we enjoyed what stimuli we received without having to actually do anything. The droll banter was pleasant and we looked forward to have someone work our scalp. But the only activity we engaged in was sporadic, casual reading. Mainly we were simply waiting – waiting for someone to do something that might be of interest. My prospects, my future, and my life, past and present, were written between invisible lines. They came perilously close to staying invisible. I could feel myself fading into life's footnotes. It feels like changing into H.G. Well's invisible man.

I've known people in their teens that could describe, if not a career ladder, then at least a final goal. As for me, well, to know the tale, know the teller.

1

Dreams begin in every way imaginable. But most of them are only flighty, momentary dreams, which exit as quickly as they came, with no real impact on the dreamer. In times past they were not dreams of being in a rock band, they were quick visions of being a world champion athlete, or of finding treasure on some long forgotten island. I know they had no lasting impact because there was no accompanying thought of the hard work it would take to make them a reality. By some magical process, the fruits of such little fantasies would be full blown without a drop of preceding sweat.

Dreams that would actually shape us require someone putting our foot on the proper path. We don't generally seem to find our way there alone. My first real dream tutor was a 5th grade teacher who introduced our class to one of America's top dream merchants, Richard Halliburton. Long before my time, he had been America's most popular author until he disappeared in a typhoon on the China Sea while sailing a Junk. He was a Princeton graduate who wrote light hearted personal adventure stories that took place in countries Americans longed to see. I still keep some of his books in my library such as "The Glorious Adventure" wherein he retraced the route of Ulysses in "The Odyssey". I've kept "The Flying Carpet" where he bought a small plane and hopped across the Sahara. Too, I've kept "New Worlds to Conquer" detailing how he swam the length of the Panama Canal. Upon being told the massive locks displacing many tons of water would only be opened for ships, he had himself registered as the U.S.S. Richard Halliburton. He would swim a few miles each day, accompanied by a rowing marksman who would keep crocodiles at a distance. But whether Halliburton was sneaking into the Taj Mahal at night or scaling the Matterhorn with no climbing experience, we thrilled at his personal pluck and vivid imagination. The written exploits of his adventures contained no edge of the seat fears, no complexities to unravel, and no tragedies. If you lived vicariously through Richard Halliburton you knew you'd win. Even situations that could turn dangerous involving nefarious characters turned benign like pirate Wallace Berry as Long John Silver in "Treasure Island". Richard Halliburton turned xenophobic Americans into foreign watchers. He reduced the supercilious education of the Ivy League into nothing more than a tiny backdrop on a large, diversified world stage. He started me thinking foreign.

When the next fog lifted, I was 16. Despite all the communications from adults to the contrary, teenage years were not fun. Maybe the grown folk overestimated us because our generation invented Rock and Roll, accepted college enrollment as a given, and were nonchalant on jobs and the A-bomb. But more often there were our own unrealized hopes, soul twisting pains, and fears we were ill equipped to face. This may not be true of today's teens, though I suspect it is. Too, it may not be found in the memory banks of those who were in envied social cliques. Yet, most of us, regardless of good looks and marvelous health, led lives of shy, dull, semi-isolation. Dreams are a tonic to thriving, but to kick start them, to conjure them, they must first have a spontaneous start, no matter how small or how unrelated to what you eventually want. Mine began while stumbling toward sanctuary.

We all looked for refuge, and in 1956, I found mine at the Avalon Art Theater. I wasn't there because my sophistication exceeded any other 16 year old. The Avalon offered films that would be considered "soft porn" had the term been coined.

Neither me, nor my pals, had ever known a girl carnally, and we were convinced that to do so would be akin to the creation of the universe. It would cure acne, lift self-concept from purgatory, and add to world peace. It would whisk away the disgusting and hurtful events of school like a high- powered leaf blower.

The Avalon was an anomaly. Every film was foreign, with sub titles. But if you fell behind in reading, you still understood the story. Sex was the pivot point.

I don't recall the Avalon having a concession stand. Anyway, who wanted popcorn with such an abundance of cheesecake?

The theater's furnishings were a bit worn, but not seedy. There were no strong smells or suspicious characters in the row before or behind. Actually, there were never many people of any description. Oddly, it was located in a blue collar, slightly deteriorating business area of Houston about three miles from home. Owning an old jalopy, distance was no bar. Unless those living nearby had been in the military, it was doubtful any of them had been overseas. The theater was simply located in the wrong place for everyone but myself and a few friends. I was always somewhat embarrassed when buying my ticket. I imagined that the woman in the booth would one day say, "Boy, I know why you're here. Why don't you go home to your Sears and Roebuck catalogue before you get into trouble?"

It was at the Avalon that I first saw Sophia Loren and Bridget Bardot. Sophia stood in the middle of traffic and slapped her male companion. He slapped her back and they dove into a heated embrace as traffic stopped, horns honked, and the movie ended. I recall thinking she should come to the U.S. where she might be a hit. I didn't understand the values or modus operandi of the actors, but that made them all the more fascinating. The men were more aggressive in their sexuality, and the women generally seemed glad of it.

One thing is certain: When the lights went out at the Avalon, magic happened. Strange music that never made the Hit Parade began. Not a single actor was known to any of us. It seemed to add to the realism when you could not relate the characters to those you had just seen in another role. They had not made the mistake of being on talk shows where you could see how vapid and boring they really are until a writer puts clever words in their mouths. They were the people they played. We were not as naive as generations before that believed Theda Bara might actually have been raised in the shadow of the Sphinx on serpent's milk. And, we would not have liked the asinine antics of today's stars whose money so far outpaces their intelligence and tastes. But, we were not so far from the crowd that lined up on the dock of Havana to greet Errol Flynn with repetitive chants of "Captain Blood."

The most memorable movie involved an overweight, not too handsome man, who stopped at a jewelry counter to chat with a rare beauty. As he and his friend walked down the street, he gave his pal a note to take back to this celebration of womanhood. The note simply said, "Meet me at the corner at 7:00. If you can't come, I'll understand." When she appeared at the corner, the note stuck in my mind as if welded. I never really understood what he would understand. Was it that she had no interest, or that she wanted to come but could not? Clearly, the words contained a spell. All skepticism aside, I have successfully used the ploy three times in my life, the last to begin the romance that resulted in my marriage.

Finally, the movie would end tragically, and the word "Fin" would flash across the screen. We would file out more ready to meet the world.

More ready because we had reaffirmed that there were other worlds out there, and we would therefore, not have to bear our own forever.

Despite monotony being built on tedium, I plowed ahead on my education, drifting around the world during summer vacations, finally becoming accustomed to what I was sure would be my life story. There was no escape from a forty-hour workweek, from an average home and a low-level, white-collar job. I would, in the end, subtract more from this world than I put in, and would go into God's eternity making no more glitch on the cosmic radar screen than a stealth jet the size of a crow. It was like a film noir with no way out. I felt as though my ego was just beneath the whale excrement at the bottom of the Marianas Trench. I was sustained as the years went by, only by Linda, who became my wife.

By my late twenties, Linda and I, who were in grad school, decided to take a most needed, brief vacation to Yucatan during school break. In 1968, Yucatan was still a remote, odd destination. Though small groups of hippies took refuge from society's mainstream on Isla Mujeres, and Jackie Kennedy had paid a brief visit, it was not most people's top pick. Those were days before Cancun or even Cozumel, as we now know them. We went to relax, yet the vacation was one that would turn into many years of self-imposed labor.

CHAPTER 2

From the air, Merida looked like buildings that had been sprinkled into a huge forest. I liked that. A city without trees is as ugly to me as a chicken without feathers.

Before the large Japanese built airport that travelers now enjoy, the terminal was a small wooden structure losing its battle with tropical mold and rot. Two dissipated customs agents quickly put a chalk mark on your luggage, passing you through.

To this day I believe, if you are heat tolerant, that Merida is one of the best tourist destinations worldwide. For starters, it is an easy city to get into and out of. I've been to many cities that were not. In Rangoon, we received police threats of jail if we dealt on the black market. In Cairo, my passport was confiscated at the hotel desk while police took several days to check me out. And from Merida it is a short distance east to Cuba, west to Mexico City, or south to Central America.

The streets of Merida are numbered rather than named, with even numbers going in one direction and odd numbers in the other. In this way, you can quickly compute, without a map, how far you must go to reach your destination. I thought this was very appropriate for a people who had once demonstrated such a talent for mathematics. We were told the Mayas had the concept of the zero even before the Romans, and that their calendar had three hundred and sixty five and one fourth days of the year, making leap year unnecessary.

This beautiful city has two main zocalos (squares) within two blocks of one another. The larger has a sixteenth century cathedral still in operation, and if you sit on one of its many benches feeding the pigeons, you will eventually see every one of its one million inhabitants. Colorful shops, hotels, and restaurants are within easy walking distance and there is never a need to take public transportation, even for the very young or very old.

The smaller square has a very large sidewalk restaurant with cheap, quick, courteous service, and the Gran Hotel. The Gran must have once been a truly grand hotel. There are no elevators but the broad stairway permits easy passage even for groups. If you use your imagination, you can see Emiliano Zapata standing at the head of the stairs reviewing the Army of the South, encamped where the sidewalk restaurant now is. Frequently, there is even xylophone music to accompany your meal or drinks.

There is never difficulty finding a room in any of the hotels since the main thrust of tourism moved into Cancun years ago. I cannot bear Cancun. While it has clear water and a good beach, it has no authenticity. The only Mexicans you will find in the American strip are those serving tourists. The Mexican town of Cancun is two miles away and exists to furnish workers for the American aisle. This strip allows college age Americans a place to get drunk in luxury and to openly do things they wouldn't do at home. It is Gomorrah on the gulf. By contrast, in Merida you rub elbows with direct descendants of the Mayas and are only as far from the real Mexico as you want to be. But while we frolicked in Merida, destiny edged me out of the driver's seat so subtly I thought I was still in control.

We were staying at the small San Jose Hotel that is modern yet with no character. I dislike places like that. It was even some six blocks from the square. We must have left the selection to the cab driver. One night there I passed an open door where an elderly lady and her husband were giving a slide lecture. Upon asking their purpose, Jeanette Westfall explained that she and her husband Bill, a physician, were part of the Alliance for Progress. They lived in Iowa and Iowa and Yucatan were partner states. Actually, the partnership included the two states of the peninsula, Campeche and Yucatan, and the territory of Quintana Roo. It was a program with lots of government encouragement, but very little money, relying mainly on volunteers. Each of our participating states selected an area in Latin America to assist in whatever way they would. Bill and Jeanette offered me a tour of the dark, hidden side of Merida the following day.

After breakfast, we went to the November 20th Hospital. It was an exact replica of its sister hospital in Havana, Cuba, built in 1946. November 20th was a charity hospital for farmers and laborers that did not qualify for treatment under Mexico's Social Security system. Payment at November 20th was on a sliding scale. Patients had to pay whatever they could. Officially the hospital had 62 doctors and 15 interns. I didn't know where they hid them, as there were very few in evidence. Perhaps some came in one day a year. There were no volunteers.

A dead dog, just to the left of the front door seemed to herald what we might expect. Inside, there were long lines of beds, some without sheets, and others with sheets stained by body fluids. Plaster was crumbling on the walls and there were no screens on the window. Flies came in at will and had to be fanned away by attending family members. There were no bells to ring for a doctor or nurse, and too few people to come even if there had been a buzzer. I thought the people who survived November 20th must have been tougher than they looked. As we walked down the hall, a woman lay groaning in her bed. One of the attendants accompanying us on our tour stuffed a sheet into the mouth of the suffering lady as if to say "be quiet, we have visitors." The hospital had malnourished babies that weighed less at the age of 6 months than when they were born. They lay in their own feces with typhoid patients several feet away. As we proceeded, an elderly woman followed me, finally begging for a Peso.

Our physician guide took us into the Intensive Care room where a small, seven year old girl had just been taken from an operation. She had tubes sticking out of her nose, and something about her melted my heart. This was all wrong. She should be playing with friends, not lying in a medical hovel attended by a skeleton staff. We had come to Merida on a holiday but the fun turned gray.

When we left the hospital, I felt changed; like a small, gullible kid who had just been told there was no Santa Claus. I reviewed my charity contributions and it seemed like too much of it went to a building payment, carpeting, office supplies, salaries, and other things too far removed from bread and the people that needed it. I wanted more mileage for my buck.

CHAPTER 3

Back at school, I began to think of the huge percentage of people of the world that live in villages. These are people who have no Social Security, no welfare, no doctors, no support system. The thought came to me that perhaps I could go into one of those villages and really make a difference. Even more grandiose, that I might construct a blueprint for others. I was vaguely aware of the massive corporate foundations that claimed to do various things, but it seemed to me as though we'd left matters to the government and companies for far too long. Maybe small-scale efforts could do something they could not, or would not. But in the entire world, where to begin?

Though there are arctic villages, I wanted to work in the tropics. There, at least, agricultural opportunities should exist. Recently coming from Yucatan, it seemed a good place to start. It was close enough to allow a quick flight home if some tropical disease befell me. I didn't realize at the time that often, tropical diseases are best treated in their country of origin. The doctors there see the diseases frequently, and can diagnose correctly and quickly.

Nevertheless, the Yucatan Peninsula is a big place. Even if my naive and slightly enlarged estimate of what I had to offer was correct, where should I begin? It was obvious I would need to do a reconnaissance once I decided more precisely what I was looking for. When I revealed my plan to classmates, some suggested that I work in the U.S. But a single large family in the U.S. could devour in two months all I was likely to raise.

After wrestling with the matter for some time, I decided that my primary requirement should be isolation. An isolated village would help me avoid government interference, and make sure money spent would remain in the village rather than going into the hands of passers-by. Secondly, I wanted a village as poor as possible. Problems are often created by those who get the basic protein; they just don't get the dessert. And I wanted a village desperate enough that they would welcome almost anyone to come in and do almost anything. Next, I wanted a small village. I imagined a village of approximately one hundred people. Too few people might result in just enriching a few families. Too many people could result in the resources being spread so thin that it would do no one any significant good. If an abundance of villages met these criteria, I would select one on the border of a state or territory in case I had to leave suddenly for political reasons.

Once my criterion for village selection was more or less lined up, finances needed consideration. I've never been a salesman and didn't want to go hat in hand to anyone. But I figured by canceling my other charity contributions and saving two hundred dollars per month, I could have about five thousand after two years. Honest to God, I don't know how I figured that amount was a relevant figure, but such was my goal.

As college students are prone to do, I devised a questionnaire, which I envisioned I would complete on each village family. It would give the names of the head of the families, list family members, their ages, and occupations, if any, their medical condition, and indications of what they had tried to uplift the family, as well as where they had succeeded and where they had failed. The forms proved useless. If I had spoken Mayan and Spanish, and had been there for a year or longer, they might have yielded some useful, or at least interesting data. But I had planned a three-month model of assistance. It was hoped that, if successful, I might outline a plan that could be duplicated by students, or faculty, between school years. Also, three months would be sufficient time to plant and see a harvest being made ready. Time spent with an interpreter however, was far too precious to waste filling out forms, which might only later yield something, when the problems of here and now are coming at you as though shot out of a wind tunnel.

After choosing a village, I would have a sizeable block of time to learn the basics of agriculture, animal husbandry, or any other skill I needed. My financial stipend commitments required that, upon graduating, I go to Wisconsin and work for two years until 1971.

While it sounds as if the tasks before me were well defined and orderly, in reality, they were often confusing and did not work as planned.

The day finally came that I graduated so we packed our meager belongings and headed north.

CHAPTER 4

Once in Wisconsin, I had a full time job and have never been a person with a high energy level. Studies on topics needed for village work were slow and often frustrating. The books I found on farm subjects all assumed that the reader knew agricultural basics and was involved in large scale farming economics. I spent valuable time learning skills I thought I might need, but as matters developed, I never used. I took a correspondence course on goat raising, as well as courses in brick laying and gas welding. It would turn out the village wanted no animals and there was no occasion to lay bricks or cement blocks. A very heavy Cinva Ram I'd bought for making blocks was given many years later to a mission in Africa. The welding gauges I took from the U.S. did not fit the Mexican tanks and the need for welding was limited and infrequent. I hired a French immigrant to show me how to prepare a chicken we bought at a local Chinese market. This was another unused skill. But like most of us, I never regretted anything I've ever learned whether I used it or not. It seems to me life is like a giant puzzle, and the more pieces you can put together, the less anxiety you have about not understanding how the world works. Part of the neurosis of modern man is that he recognizes that he depends on machines and systems that he doesn't understand. I began compiling a loose-leaf notebook with basics on cattle, goats, chickens, composting, fishponds, fruit trees, soybeans, soil testing, water purification, and every other pioneering topic.

To fill in my vast reservoir of ignorance and being city raised, I talked to anyone I found at the Laundromat or other gathering places, who might have had farm experience. I picked up more than a little misinformation.

When asked if hens need roosters to lay eggs, one woman said "yes", while another told me they need roosters to start them off, but not thereafter. No one had an idea of a good ratio of roosters to hens; so I thought couples would be nice. I later learned that five roosters for ninety-five hens are sufficient and that hens never need roosters to lay eggs. Roosters are only needed for fertile eggs to hatch chicks. And it seemed amazing to me to find that the period from laying to hatching, regardless of the bird, is usually 21 or 22 days.

I took Spanish I three times, never once finishing. Few things are more mentally laborious than the, devoid of logic, rote memorization of foreign language study. Still, since Spanish uses the same alphabet with a few modifications, I was not without success altogether. To this day, I do not speak Spanish, but I have many words thereof, and am grateful for every one. One Spanish teacher said, "Some Americans think that to speak Spanish, all you have to do is add an 'o' or an 'e' at the end of every word." While in Mexico City he heard two Americans order 'Tea-o frió (pronunciation in Spanish would be Tio frió). He said that literally means 'cold uncle.' When asked what they were served, the teacher looked a little taken aback and said, "iced tea." Mexicans are quite accustomed to our butchering their language and are very tolerant. I believe they appreciate any attempts we make. For the beginner, it is mainly important that you speak loud enough to be audible, and that you give yourself permission to make mistakes. The most valuable first words I learned were "yo necessito" (I need). To that I could add a long list of nouns. I took a chance that I wouldn't need the usual phrases put forth in language books, even the "I demand to see the American Consul."

Fortunately, my search for farm moxie happily coincided with the beginning of a large movement of our young returning to the land. Hippies morphed into first time farmers, often as part of a commune, and the publishing world moved to meet their needs. My successful search for written instructions began with "The Whole Earth Catalogue." It was a large paper back volume which named and reviewed books which would help keep greenhorns from starving when they shucked their city jobs for a piece of bare ground. These books gave the most elementary advice on bee keeping, rabbit raising, log cabin building, and finding security with five acres of land. "Mother Earth News" came along as an interesting supplement, if not an always-complete manual. The catalogue also gave sources for non-electrical tools, exotic seeds, windmills, pumps, composting, delivering babies, and virtually everything a frontiersman would need to know. Along with my book purchases, I obtained copies of the Air Force and Army survival manuals. I joked with friends that I had a library that would be worth millions if we had to start civilization all over again. My library could bring us up to the nineteenth century. It included a book on doing village work in Papua, New Guinea, one on village work in the Philippines, "The Barefoot Doctor's Manuel" of China, the "ABC's of Beekeeping," "Five Acres and Independence," "Three acres and Security," a "Village Technology Handbook," and "Living the Good Life" by Helen and Scott Nearing. I studied methods of purification of water (e.g. charcoal, sand filters, boiling, chlorine, Halazone tablets, and iodine drops).

CHAPTER 5

The year following our vacation to Yucatan was time to do a reconnaissance. My dad, who greatly loved to travel, came with me on this fact-finding mission.

As we drove out from Merida, we saw large henequen plantations, apparently abandoned. Henequen, or Sisal, had been quite valuable for rope production before World War Two, but with the invention of synthetics, such as nylon, the market collapsed. The terrain of Yucatan is chiefly low lying and flat, with a thin layer of soil atop deep layers of porous limestone. As the early explorers noted, the trees are almost all about the same height, looking as though someone had gone across the top with giant scissors. Everything looked very dry and parched. Nowhere in Yucatan is there a lake or river. I wondered how many early explorers died of thirst looking for a source of water. There are however, cenotes. A cenote is a place where a circular chunk of earth's surface has collapsed, exposing the vast lake that underlies the peninsula. It is this underground lake that gives Merida, and the other towns, their water. Even the Well of Death at Chichen-Itza and countless villages draw from this.

There were also massive chicken houses that had been abandoned. We drove many miles and visited some remote towns using a large aerial map I had bought at the American Book Store in Mexico City. One such village was called Tabi that was isolated and the size I sought, but had received enough Presbyterian assistance to insure they would make it. The State of Campeche was simply too busy for our purposes. Except by air, one could not get into Merida from the north without going through

Campeche. We found Quintana Roo, then a territory, too distant from any supply market. In the old days a rough crowd called chicleros went through the jungle of the territory seeking gum from the chiclero trees for chewing gum. Annually they would throw a massive party, which attracted pistoleros and prostitutes from all over Mexico. Perhaps a dozen men would be killed in the drunken festivities. It seemed our search would have to focus on the State of Yucatan. Yet all the towns and villages we saw were too large, excepting a single-family settlement. At one point, we had taken a wrong turn and the further we went, the more the scrub jungle closed in around us. What had started as a rough road became a rougher trail. I had to use the Volkswagen Beetle as a battering ram to turn around. We lost some chrome, but with no radiator and the engine in the rear, nothing mechanical was harmed. Later, we were told that if we had continued about three miles on the trail, it would have ended where an old man lived with his sons. It seems to me that he must have wanted to escape his fellow man something awful to go to such a place. To the armchair adventurer, the jungle looks exciting and luxuriant. I've learned it hides many miseries. It conceals strange deadly diseases, great poverty, and a daily battle with nature. It is the last place on earth most people would want to spend their vacation. The heat is stifling, and even the animals that live there are infested with parasites. Monkeys catch three times the variety of Malaria men do, and an autopsy on any wild creature will reveal worms. Even the soil is usually poor and is quite often laterite. Laterite is highly mineralized soil that is good so long as it is covered with a thick layer of leaf mold. However, when it is exposed to the air, as plowing does, it begins to turn to stone. Many ancient temples are built of laterite. Too often the soil of the jungle will grow what is already there and little else.

While the trip gave us an overall view of the state, and a fair idea of where we did not want to go, we returned home failing in our principle mission. I had talked with, or later sent letters to, sixteen priests, missionaries and low-level government workers explaining that I was looking for a village to plow some five thousand dollars into, yet they had no recommendations. I don't know whether the tropical sun had sautéed their motivation or they simply didn't believe me. I did not realize that a seed had been planted.

It was disappointing to know another reconnaissance would have to be done. Even so, some months after I had returned to Milwaukee, I received a hand written letter from a New Yorker who had gone to Yucatan to "recover from Schizophrenia". He wrote that he had heard I was looking for a village to help and wondered if I would consider one named Yaxachen. While there, he had married a Mayan woman and had "gone native" as was said. He gave me some stories of what a grueling life the people of Yaxachen had and how small was their hope. I sent him back a couple of letters asking questions about the village but only received fragments of answers. Obviously, his alternate cure for schizophrenia had not worked. But I put Yaxachen on the top of my list for a visit when I returned. Wherever he is today, I pray God will rest his tortured mind, a feat beyond mankind.

CHAPTER 6

On the second reconnaissance, I went alone, excepting an interpreter I had found in Merida's main square. We drove about ninety miles inland through Muna and Ticul, to a large trade center called Oxkutzcab which is on any detailed map of Yucatan. The road to Oxkutzcab was good except that we had to proceed through many towns, and do so slowly since they were protected by constant topes (speed bumps). Today, there is a loop that bypasses these towns, but then, it was one long, kidney jarring experience.

Oxkutzcab, then and now, was a town of about twenty thousand. Its most distinguishing feature is a large, open-air produce market in its center. I wondered how most people made a living there. I still wonder. As then, it has a couple of male only bars, a splendid, but poorly patronized restaurant, some government offices, the traditional sixteenth century church still functioning, a CONASUPO store (where the government subsidizes prices on basic foods), and a few nondescript offices.

We were told to turn right on Calle Forty Four, just after half circling the square, and that the road would lead us into a tiny town called Xul near Yaxachen. To my amazement, the road that led to Xul was paved. About 5 miles after leaving Oxkutzcab, is the cave of Lol Tun, which was later developed as a thinly visited tourist site. The cave of Lol Tun is a large cathedral cave with cave paintings some ten thousand years old. It has two stalactites that are hollow. When one strikes them, they make a musical sound. Towards the end of the cave, a large chunk of what had been the roof was broken through and a massive tree grows through the roof in heliotropic manner toward the sun.

Mainly, we were told there was a paved road to Xul because an ex-governor had his hacienda beyond Xul. The road was good, but narrow and curving, gently moving upward for the next 12 miles. The vegetation around the serpentine road grew ever heavier, so I found myself frequently honking the horn to alert any vehicle coming in our direction that I could not see. Still, we passed no one.

Sometimes we would see a burnt out patch of land. The Mayans do this, as their forefathers did, to clear space for farming. While it adds potash to the soil, it is detrimental in other ways. There is no companion crop planting, and overwhelmingly, the main crop grown is corn. When a particular patch of land is exhausted, they merely move on and repeat the process elsewhere.

"Xul", in Mayan, means "the end" as it was the end of Mayan world. This end of this old world was too small for many surprises. The few people stared at us, marking them as ones who rarely received visitors. The town had only the ruins of a centuries old church and a few huts along the road. "We were told a bus came through once a week. The road we had traveled continued on out of sight, and in many years I have never used it past Xul. We were told that the road to Yaxachen began at the far end of a large open area that served as a square.

The "road" to Yaxachen started bad, and quickly grew worse. The only vehicles that ever traveled it were the heavy government trucks that brought water to Yaxachen in times of drought.

Though the road was cleared of vegetation, there were rocks of all sizes everywhere, pointed ones, large ones, and angled ones. There were a few relatively navigable spots on the road and while on one of these, I grew over confident, proceeding too fast, and rocks punched their way through the rear seat floorboard and into the battery. Thereafter, we had to shove the car off to get it started. For much of the trip someone had to walk in front of the car telling the driver which way to cut the wheels. During another impatient moment, to escape a torturous pace, I made a brief sprint, which resulted in the car being suspended dead center on a rock. Not a wheel was touching the ground. The lightness of the Beetle really paid off when it came time to shove it.

At long last we came to a tiny grouping of houses I thought to be Yaxachen. It turned out to be only a couple of families living nearer their milpas (corn farm). The settlement's Mayan name was Xobenhaltun. We pressed on and a little later finally came into Yaxachen. It was the end of the road, the end of my energy, and the end of our patience. And truly, at Yaxachen, we seemed to be at the end of the world. Everyone came out of their huts to see, and in some cases, to touch us. Not knowing what else to do, I asked to speak to the official in charge. That turned out to be Commissario Laureano. He was a short, powerfully built man, handsome of features and quiet and polite. With him came a group of the other prominent men in the village. I suggested a town hall meeting and while they rounded up as many folks as would fit within the tiny, one room cement schoolhouse, I toured the village. Like towns everywhere in Mexico, it had an open space in the center. At the edge of the square near the town well, was a large holding tank that Presbyterians had constructed years ago. It had taps along the bottom but went unused. Water was so difficult to get out of the village well that no one wanted to store their hard wrought supply in a holding tank where anyone could siphon it. The Presbyterians had flown in, built the tank, inoculated the village, and flew out. I never saw them return. Later, the holding tank was to prove very useful.

Water was obtained from the only well by using a huge, archaic wooden spool standing ten feet high. Eight men could get on the end of a pole, extending from the spokes of the spool, and by turning the spool sixteen times in one direction, lower eight 5 gallon cans to a depth of three hundred feet. By going sixteen times in the opposite direction, it raised forty gallons of water. The spool changed the direction of the pull but gave no mechanical advantage that I could see. It was backbreaking work. The well itself was about 4 ft in diameter, and no one knows who or how it was dug, straight down through limestone. Beside the well was a large piece of equipment of an unknown purpose. I took down the serial number noting that it was manufactured in Milwaukee, Wisconsin. When I returned to Milwaukee, I called the company and was told it was a "power take off clutch." I did not ask for a tutorial on its use.

Houses in Yaxachen were all essentially the same. They were one-room huts with dirt floors and two large parallel poles inside used to hang hammocks. Hammocks are the only way to sleep in such heat. Unlike the traditional U.S. hammocks that are of one piece, the Yucatan hammocks are made of many slender threads, which allow the air to circulate beneath you. The multiple slender threads design keeps the hammocks from flipping on you, as one-piece hammocks are prone to do. Anyone who lived before air conditioning can tell you of summer's miseries in a bed. Even as a slender child I can recall how the spot on which you laid would quickly become heated so you'd have to revolve to another place on the mattress. You were like a chicken on a constantly revolving rotisserie, getting a better workout in bed than when you arose for the day's activities. Various techniques were tried to thwart the heat, none very effective. Even older homes with high ceilings, which allowed the heat someplace to go, were miserable from June to September. People in the South would sometimes take their mattress to the front porch or would wet towels to press against themselves. Fans mainly circulated hot air and even the glorious attic fans were primarily of utility in the Fall and Spring. Trees helped slightly, but whoever called them "nature's air conditioners" was certainly guilty of hyperbole. I think with minimal marketing, Yucatecan hammocks would have sold like snow cones on a hot U.S. summer day. While their market offered even children's hammocks, I loved the large, matrimonial hammocks. Sleeping perpendicular to the direction of the hammock allows you to sleep flat and avoid sore heels the following day. Only with the hammock was I able to actually sleep in the heat of the day. The huts are built oblong in the old, Mayan fashion. At one end would be some stones to make a stovetop. As a single piece of furniture, a hut might have a simple wooden chair. There would be no sign of a change of clothes, of tools, of food, or of toys for children. Some homes were bordered by a loosely piled stone fence. The walls of the huts are saplings of irregular size, which allow a limited view of the inhabitants inside.

The "streets" if you were generously inclined to call them such, all radiated from the square. They led nowhere, only allowing residents to walk to one another's hut.

Yaxachen looked and smelled poor. I can now, always tell a real village from a Hollywood set. Everywhere there were cornhusks and the smell of animal excrement. When the rains came, there was no drainage and people would sometimes walk in water calf deep that had been fouled by various substances.

At this, our first of many meetings, I asked how many people lived in Yaxachen. "Four hundred" was their answer. I decided on the spot that four hundred was as close as I was likely to come to my ideal without an endless string of reconnaissance missions. The officials asked why I would be interested in helping them. I simply stated all men are brothers.

Since so many of us were crammed into such a small, hot, dark place, I gave them the barest idea of what I had in mind and asked them what they needed help in doing. One of the men, Santiago, said, "If you will help us with a pump and the road, you will be remembered as gods". I later made the misstep of telling that to a Houston reporter, whose article was entitled, "Houstonian's deeds make him a 'god'." I thought that was a potent invitation to return, and somewhat amusing. Yet after the article, friends began to blame me for the weather, why they didn't get a raise, etc. and I searched for a place to resign godship.

The people of Yaxachen passed on my offer to bring them animals, as fetching water for these would be too difficult.

At the close of the meeting, I told them I would return in one year with money, equipment, and people to help. They softly spoke "Bueno" but I do not believe, for a minute, that they believed me. For seven years, the Mexican government had promised a pump for their well, the promises usually coming just before elections. About the only thing marking my visit as any different, was a pack filled with rapport building gifts. These included medicines, dried foods, and vitamins.

After I had given out the treats, before we could board our vehicle and leave, I was approached by a man whose wife was having terrible stomach pains - looking back; I wish I would have taken her with us to a proper doctor, perhaps in Oxkutzcab. Maybe I did not want to begin any work with a death, I do not recall. Or perhaps, I had seen too many movies where the doctor was threatened with death if he did not save the life of a prominent villager. As fate would have it, I had one item left – Alka Seltzer. I gave directions for its use, said a silent prayer for a placebo effect, and quickly drove off. So I returned to the United States with a target village selected. It was a good feeling. For the whole of my plan could be divided into four stages; (1) saving the money, (2) learning the needed skills, (3) selecting the village, and (4) doing the work therein. I believed the first three stages were in the bag.

CHAPTER 7

Once back in the U.S. I realized things had worked well. My agreement with the State of Wisconsin, which had paid for my schooling, had been for two years. So the following year, 1971, I would be free for three months, or as long as it took. My preparations escalated.

Not knowing what I could find in foreign markets or how long it would take me to find what would be needed, I began to buy foods and equipment. For foods, I concentrated on items which were dried, light and compact, with a long shelf life, that did not require cooking. Through a mail order company, I bought two cast iron hand cranked grinders of corn. I thought a village without electricity would surely need these. Later I was to learn that the village storeowner, Feliciano, had a fuel driven corn grinder and did the work for the entire village for a tiny percentage. On a reconnaissance you can never collect too much information, and often miss things.

I learned that hand lift pumps are only good for a maximum of twenty-two feet and that windmills require a seven-mile per hour wind. Windmills were particularly disappointing since I know much of rural America had low amounts of electricity supplied to their farms by the "Delco System". In this system, lights would be run off of batteries, and while the windmill recharged the batteries, it pumped water as well. I found a kerosene-operated refrigerator but it was prohibitively expensive. I came onto a good formula for making your own soap, but it would be lye soap, soft, and without modern fragrances. Too, given modern transportation and wide availability of markets, buying soap seemed to be the easiest course. At a chemical company I found "water glass" which is supposed to preserve eggs even longer than refrigeration. However, given the life span of an egg among hungry people, it did not seem relevant either. I found some nitrogen fixing bacteria to roll the bean seeds in since they would be grown in an area where no beans had previously been planted. I was told that would noticeably improve the first crop.

I also started to accumulate medicines and, in the fullness of time, found kindly physicians that would give me their out of date samples. Unless the medicines are drastically out of date they should be fine. Even though Mexico usually doesn't require a prescription, free meds are quite a perk. I gave a lot of thought to the heat I would be facing in the tropics, but came up with little. I knew enough to take salt as needed, to keep from becoming dehydrated, and to hide from the sun at its peak. I recalled an article written by a doctor in Houston over one hundred years ago. He wrote, "At noon, all we do is lie underneath a tree and pant." I figured the Yucatan sun deserved at least as much respect as Houston's.

To add to my knowledge, I sent hundreds of letters to seed companies, the Department of Health, Education, and Welfare (who would refer whatever question I had to the appropriate department and eventually answer me), and to organizations like Volunteers for International Technical Assistance (VITA), a group which gave free advice to those doing charity work abroad.

Mainly, I can say that the project occupied almost every hour apart from my day job. I kept a box beneath my bed with a pencil and pad by the lamp. Sometimes, in the middle of the night, I would get what seemed like a clever idea. Without leaving bed, I could jot the brainstorm down and stuff it in the box and return to sleep. I would have been embarrassed for anyone to have seen some of those ideas, and I would, in the light of day, cull many of them. I had a loose-leaf notebook crammed with topics and notes on all.

In preparation, I stepped up my daily exercise routine. I was almost thirty years old and was no trainee. Still I saw to it that I could run a mile and do forty pushups on demand. I had already learned that even standard tourist travel is more enjoyable if you are in a modicum of condition. Gradually, I began to trade general philosophies and theories for specific skills and useful information.

For the first time in my life, I had a truly worthy project all my own. It was not a part of an organization that someone else had begun. It was not one that society had carved out which would lead to a work world living, nor was it a prerequisite to earning a rank or privilege. It paid nothing, yet it consumed me. I began to see that the happiest people in life are those who lose themselves in some cause bigger than greedy self. For some it had been the communist party, for others a freedom fight, and for some Christianity. I avoided looking too closely at my own motives. There was a great need and I wanted to respond to that need. Introspection could lead to no good. Only by keeping it simple could I be sure of surviving assaultive examination from within as well as from without. I would concentrate on filling stomachs, curing diseases, building a road, and getting a water pump.

Financially, I had no problem saving the two hundred dollars per month I had originally planned, as well as buying much material. To have yet more money to put back into the effort, I formed a small, non-profit organization. I was not aware that this did not put me on the IRS list of tax-deductible organizations. That proved more difficult. As the years passed, IRS requirements expanded and finally I closed down the organization. This was both because of my age and because the juice no longer seemed worth the squeeze. The IRS personnel however, were consistently helpful and courteous.

Outside of my salary, I received help from two entities. One was the Milwaukee Public School System. Every year their Industrial Arts Department held an auction to be rid of tools and kitchen equipment that were either worn or obsolete by design. Teachers bidding on the equipment would engage in bickering that would end in personal rancor. To preserve harmony and help a good cause, the man in charge sold me the entire stock for twenty dollars. It included institutional cooking pots, large lots of plastic eating bowls, and tools including planes, vices and such. The other assisting entity was the Partners of the Alliance, which paid my mileage to the village. The village selection, the timing, the financing all seemed to occur by accident. Now, I no longer believe that. In retrospect, the sequence worked so perfectly.

I devised about half a dozen programs to get the villagers involved in, reasoning we would let programs they did not support collapse, and put our full weight behind those they did support. With such a short-term model in mind, I wanted to hit the ground running. As matters turned out, neither the programs, nor the time frame, unfolded as I expected. Once in the village, both were trumped by the well-defined needs the villagers expressed, and by my financial limitations.

I had no idea how many Americans I might need to help me, so I proceeded on the maxim "the more the better". This too was a mistake as events developed. I underestimated what the villagers could do for themselves given a little financial help. And an interpreter is a conduit through which almost all communication must be funneled. Interpreting is slow and complicated. A ratio of only three people to one interpreter would have been more realistic. By the time we were ready to go to work, I had recruited two young women and four young men. They seemed idealistic and eager for adventure. None appeared to have particularly relevant skills, but they were all bright, motivated folk and I wanted as many ideas as possible.

I had been told by Jeanette that if I sent a detailed list of equipment six weeks in advance to be taken in, to their Mexican contacts, papers would be waiting for me at the border to permit this. I dutifully complied.

My plan was to rent the largest U-Haul truck available, pack in the goods I had accumulated, and we males would begin the journey to my parents' home in Houston. The ladies would fly to Houston and join us. My dad loaned me a pickup, a trailer, and a Volkswagen bus to haul the equipment to the village. He, and my oldest friend, would even go along to help us with the delivery and return in the Volkswagen bus.

Our rented truck was so crammed with materials that the two males who could not fit in the cab had to practically hang out the back with the overhead slide door being tied up for air circulation.

We got to Houston without incident and transferred some of the material to the trailer and some into the van. The remainder had to go into a pickup. To minimize the appearance of the load, we ran two by four boards the length of the camper roof and attached them. We then put material between the two by four boards and put nice paneling over it to help hold it in place. We even removed the springs from behind the seats to have room to pack things there.

So when we headed for Matamoros, we had a Volkswagen Van, trailer, and the pickup fully packed. Considering that we had nine people, we thought we might be able to cross as tourists who travel heavy, if the guards did not look too closely. When entering another country, I generally indicate to Immigration I plan to stay for several months, which can make a large load of "personal" luggage seem more realistic. If the custom's agent had ever asked about things a tourist normally does not carry, I would candidly state that I want to help as many people as possible. Everything taken must be critically viewed in terms of its weight and utility. The only thing I take which has no practical value is a book about people caught in desperate, horrible conditions such as "Babi Yar". My own comparably better circumstances help to steady my nerves.

We got to Matamoros but customs would not allow us to pass with so much material. There were none of the promised papers waiting for us. We crossed back into the U.S. and I made a frantic call to Jeanette who made some calls and was told it would take a couple of more days. We waited, using valuable funds. The arrangement I had made with the volunteers was that I would house and feed them, but pay no salaries. After a couple of days, there were still more promises but no papers. I knew Jeanette was doing all she could. She too had been taken in by childish promises with no substance. We tried crossing the border at the midnight shift with a change of guard, and tried bribes, but still had no luck. I made the gut wrenching decision to leave a substantial amount of materials behind. We rented a storage facility and left the trailer after reshuffling the goods once again, leaving the bulkier, less vital material. The following year I managed to get everything I had left behind in, but it was exasperating. I could not understand why the customs agents were so indifferent to the plight of their own people and why the government, time after time, blocked charity efforts. It was not only us. While waiting, I had contacted the Salvation Army, the American Consulate and anyone who would listen, but they had their own problems in border crossings.

With the lighter load we passed through customs. I don't know if the agents finally had a little pity on us, or if the load was that substantially smaller. Leaving during the early part of the rainy season we would encounter some rain everyday. Some goods got wet despite the tarp. Yet a tarp also serves the function of not allowing the curious to see what you are hauling.

Before the toll roads, a trip to Merida fully loaded, would take about six days. We would stop at roadside places for lunch and camping, and we made a brief excursion to Palenque. Palenque is one set of ruins that should not be missed. We would frequently be rained on and would sometimes make up lost time in foolish maneuvers. Going through the curving roads in the mountains, in the dark, I would sometimes rely on the lights of an on-coming car to let me know if I could pass slow moving trucks. This led one of the young men when we stopped to say, "You're crazy". He was right.

The costal route to Yucatan was slower but more direct. En route we stopped at Catemaco for the night. I was informed in later years that Catemaco was a witch center. But that night, beside the lake, it was beautiful camping. The town plaza was well lit and the girls were walking in a circular direction while the boys, in an outer ring, were walking in the opposite direction assessing the girls. It doubtless supplied a spark, which often led to matrimony. In general, the coastal section of the route to Yucatan was torturous. It was on heavily trafficked roads, full of potholes. So different from today where driving in Mexico on the toll roads is most pleasant once you have cleared the cities. Failure to use the expensive toll roads will put you behind every beer and pipe truck, all going 20 mph.

When we arrived in Merida, a Mexican angel named Lina Lopez de Esquivel, a friend of Jeanette's, and the wife of a hospital director, set about to help us quickly hire an interpreter. She took us to the Kennedy School of English (now out of business) where we interviewed their two prize pupils (a girl and a boy) and Lina wisely reasoned that the girl's parents might well balk at her being off in the jungle for a long period with a group of foreigners. Both were fifteen years old. We selected Jorge Cabrera Ake. His English was not great, but he was delighted to work for five dollars a day. His parents were barely in his life, and he needed only to go to his house, fetch his hammock and a change of clothes. Jorge took us to a large city market store where we bought hammocks for all of us along with the rope to string them. We also walked to a wholesale pharmacy supply and got a large box of assorted medicines that the pharmacist recommended. Lastly, we went to a wholesale food market where beans and rice were bought in two hundred and twenty pound bags along with a large supply of powdered milk and baby food. Some of these we heaped on top of the truck, tied down, and at last proceeded to the village looking like the Joad family in "Grapes of Wrath". Right when we thought perhaps the tires would pop we stopped at Oxkutzcab and bought fresh fruit.

CHAPTER 8

After the sun has set in the scrub jungle of Yucatan, it became hard to remember rooms alive with electricity and a tub filled with hot sudsy water. Dirt covers everything except clear skies laden with stars that disappeared long ago in industrialized countries. And the darkness below is unbroken by neon advertisements. It reminded me of the giant ferris wheel at the Prater in Vienna where one could view the edge of the now gone communist world when his ferris car was in the highest position. The communists frowned on advertising so at night it was as though their terrain was under a blackout.

We pulled into Yaxachen just as the sun set. We arrived after the village had experienced one of their frequent crop failures and there was a drastic need. If we thought we had gawks before we found new meaning to the word. It was as though Barnum and Bailey had come to a dusty frontier town at the same time as Santa Claus and the Wells Fargo wagon. We were all tired so I immediately made arrangements to have our hammocks strung in whatever huts they assigned. The villagers vacated two huts to house us. No arrangements were made to separate the sexes. The ladies were shown where there were a couple of outdoor privies though normally the toilet in a village is the pig-sty. Huts were marked as having been sprayed by the government. We had no problem with mosquitos, for except after heavy rains, there was no standing water.

That night we bedded down with everything still packed and no worries about being burglarized. The people were generally related to one another. Fortunately this meant when you helped one, you helped several.

Yaxachen had no jail, no police, and you could park anywhere since there were no other cars.

We settled in with a couple of pigs grunting, some very thin dogs barking, people speaking the unintelligible Mayan just outside our doors, and every star in the universe winking at us. Soon we were awakened by little Jorge, who wanted to sleep in our hut. He claimed his had too many spiders.

We awoke the next morning in a flurry of activity. In fact, we moved too quickly. Before the day was out we had hired two men to build a latrine (a short trench with boards to sit on), had set up a field kitchen, and began dispensing food while seeing patients. This led to some confusion but it was a good, natural confusion. Things were being done and the doing was announced everywhere. The time of promises, of words, was being shattered like glass, and a cheerful wind was blowing through the holes made.

I hired up to fifty men a day (though usually a number half of this) before the first week had passed, at $1.00 per diem which was about 25% more than they normally received. I used most of them to work on their own road, but a handful began clearing a large garden. We had brought a little equipment for these purposes but when they were given jobs, wheelbarrows, pickaxes, shovels, and sledgehammers appeared from out of nowhere. The Comissario, at our request, appointed a foreman and they immediately marched off to the first cash job some of them ever had. They were paid at the end of each day, which is the only proper way to pay manual laborers. In the U.S. I've seen too many receive no pay at the end of a hard day, the employer excusing himself by saying he pays at the end of the job. If a worker with no rights receives no money after one day's work, what guarantee does he have he'll receive anything after 3 or more days? They were hard workers and really only needed instructions on which rocks were dangerous for motor vehicles and which were benign. Each day they would assemble at daybreak and without commotion, report to the road. Roadwork was not easy during the rainy season. It rained a bit each day though rarely came a downpour. Often the rain was just enough to cool down hot, sweaty bodies. I would often go and work beside them for half a day or work in the nearby garden. I quickly learned to never drink the soft drinks from the small store unless it was mineral water. Mexicans prefer more sugar in their soft drinks. That required water to displace the sugar. If you drink their soft drinks in the AM heat, you found yourself wanting one after another. After some days had passed, their foreman came to see me and said they needed dynamite for some of the more difficult areas. I gave him money for a case. There were limitations to using sledgehammers at iron bars to breaking rocks to fill in the spots. He said we would need permission from the Regional Commissario at Oxkutzcab. Well I had already had my fill of process people, being an outcome person, so I told him to forget the Commissario and just bring back the dynamite. He did so the next day. One of the advantages of being isolated is that even the dogs of the officials in Oxkutzcab, 22 miles away, could not hear our blasting. At that time I did not know how to use dynamite, but they did. They knew a great deal more than I had imagined they would. It figures that you could not be too thick and survive in their environment. For this reason alone, I should have taken fewer volunteers. Another reason curiously appeared. The males and females grew to resent one another though I never got a handle on why this was. I simply felt too hard pressed by day-to-day problems to become embroiled in what I considered an emotional regression to elementary school squabbles. Even so, they all worked and worked well. I am sure I am partly to blame for discord. Realizing that all of us are smarter than any of us, I took as many as would volunteer. There was no attempt to ascertain or match personalities, and my orientation was poor. I am better at planning in my head than at sharing the plan with others. They did not know their role and I did not know what to expect from them. And God knows young people are volatile. The ladies, without being asked, fell into doing the cooking for the group and some laundry. The men either worked on the road or in the garden along side the villagers. I had a compost bin built and one of the men got stung by a scorpion in the pile. While there was an initial pinprick, after that he claimed it gave him a high sensation. Some of the volunteers had been bitten by redbugs in a girth by their belt as they slept in their hammocks. The bites went unnoticed until they began to itch the following morning. We asked the locals what they did to prevent this and they brought out broad leaves with a sticky side up and placed them underneath the hammocks. I asked what good this did and Jorge said, "If the insect leaps on you from the ground and misses, he falls onto the leaf, gets stuck, and cannot try again." Because the dogs were treated so shabbily,

I took one of the bald, hungry Chihuahuas to sleep in my hammock with me. I called him 'mi hijo' (my son). The villagers would laugh outside my door at night. There would frequently be people talking among themselves who I suppose merely wanted to be near the action if I was to kickstart any. When I needed quiet, I would simply say: "Por favor, necissito domir" (Please, I need sleep). They would mutter something polite and drift off. Sometimes pigs looking for something to eat would bust through barriers and come into the hut. I knew from the beginning that I would be too short in the village to effectively change dysfunctional cultural traditions. When I left, the women would still have too little status for example. But like the British, I positively howl when I see an animal mistreated. In the front of my stay, it seemed an enjoyable sport to take a small rock and throw it to hear a dog yelp. I stopped that every time I saw it and before long, as I could determine, this activity disappeared altogether. While the animals are somewhat competitors for food and there is never likely to be a pampered apartment dog among them, in later years they would ask me for dog or cat food for their animals. The dogs used for hunting always looked in good condition. There were a few loose chickens in the village. They had few feathers, looked tough and I doubt they ever laid an egg. I should have pent them, and brought hen scratch and laying mash to them. Doubtless they'd have notably improved. Good nutrition and cleanliness would have solved many a problem for villagers and animals.

One of the things they wanted was cement to build a small city hall office building. I bought 17 tons of bags, which were trucked in, and before long a city hall was begun. The city hall provided for the recording of marriages and births. In later years, a new school was built by the Mexican government so pupils could move out of the tiny, one room school at the square to a modem looking elementary school about a mile away. The Mexican government is good at building edifices, but seems to give little thought as to how to staff them. A teacher did appear because of his commitment to work off his student loan, similar to our government's procedure of forgiving student loans if, upon graduation, the student is willing to teach in disadvantaged areas. A small clinic was built in Xul nine and one half miles away, but there were no medicines to put in it, and no doctors or nurses to staff it. It fell into disuse. While the elementary school looked very similar to those in the U.S. and allowed the pupils to go through the sixth grade rather than just the third, there was no water to run to the toilets, and only one teacher was available at any given time. School supplies were also at a dearth. In recognition of the extreme heat I often wonder if it would not be better to build schools and other buildings on concrete with no side walls, or walls that would roll up and down, allowing the wind to blow through.

While working on the road or in the garden, we would sometimes siesta when the sun was at its zenith. During one siesta period, we were told that there was a Bruja (witch) that lived near the bottom of the well in one of the lateral caves. I saw a rare chance to explode a myth. Those opportunities do not come every day. I asked that they lower me with the well rope where upon I would report what I saw. However, one of the volunteers wisely pointed out that I was the one with the money and plan, and that if anything happened to me, the whole operation would collapse. He volunteered himself. Slowly, he was lowered two hundred and ninety feet to the lateral caves and came back and reported no witch was home. Two of the villagers wanted to see for themselves and were lowered in return. There was no more talk of a witch. Contrary to preserve-the-culture professors, they evidenced no problem from the myth eradication. It seemed to me all cultures are changing, and they should be no more deprived of the ability to sift and lift then we are. The Greeks did not suffer from the first men, climbing Mt. Olympus who subsequently testified no gods lived there.

For $1.00 a villager made me a beautiful sapling shower curtain that could have sold for $100.00 at Pier 1. I had brought a plastic shower but the holes were so small, they quickly clogged with dirt and it was of no use. I would have done better to take a pump up pressure tank as it is used for spraying. Years later, I tried one and it worked well. Then however, bath time was when it rained heavily. I would go into the open in Bermuda shorts, lather down, and let nature rinse me. The villagers would stand in their doorway and laugh. None ever joined me despite my having passed out cases of bar soap. I can only assume they had drawn a connection between getting cold and getting sick. After the rains, it would sound as if an army of frogs were just outside of sight. Yet I saw only one frog during any trip to and from the village. I told them some people eat cooked frog legs but they simply laughed. While even after the rain I found no mosquitoes, gnats would sometimes come out in force. We had hoped to be models of hygiene, but in no time we were filthier than the villagers who were adept at sponge baths.

I had an almost football field sized area cleared for a garden where the villagers told us we could plant, and hired a half dozen men to plant the many, varied seeds I'd brought. I rolled the bean seeds in nitrogen fixing bacteria and was later told they had a nice sized crop. It was quite different from the usual technique of burning off a field and using a long pointed stick to punch a hole in the ground, then putting a kernel of corn into the hole. Then after a few years, the soil would become depleted and the farmer would move to another location and repeat the process. Corn was so exclusively the crop that even babies would be given a milk-appearing broth from the corn instead of the needed milk.

Work went well in the garden except my attempt at composting. HEW had informed me that composting was not relevant to the tropics, but I had read "The Encyclopedia of Composting" and did not listen. I had a fine compost bin built and put men with machetes to chopping and shredding the vegetation that went into it. Wasn't shredding the secret to quick composting in the U.S.? I knew I had gone wrong when after three days, instead of three weeks, the vegetation had turned black and the pile heated up. If I had it to do over I would have simply thrown un-shredded vegetation atop the ground as mulch.

Another main effort was the medical clinic we ran. When people understood that we had medicine and were not charging fees, they came in ever-larger numbers. Chiefly I handled this project. Since malnutrition and hunger seemed so often to be wedded to their ailments, we would often send them away with a few pounds of beans and rice as well as vitamins. Someone may have faked an illness to get food, but it is doubtful since they had only to ask the food dispenser to receive the same. There were frequent, out of clinic requests for a modest amount of money for such things as transportation costs to Merida, for an operation, money to fill a specialized prescription given to them by a doctor there, etc. I virtually always complied. I did not want anyone to go away empty handed; they had done that quite enough in their lives. But even when there was no help for the situation, they were polite and submissive. I made no attempt to keep records in giving out medicines or supplies of any kind. The need and requests came too rapidly for that. I did delegate, as aid given from more than one source has a better chance of not being hoarded by the few.

The village was a place where people, particularly children, died of common ailments such as whooping cough. I was glad to give them some medical access. The medical clinic grew larger as the crowds built. I felt a little like I imagined Jesus must have felt - overwhelmed. Far worse however, was the nature of the ailments brought to us. They steadily grew worse. At one point a lady brought a small baby wrapped in a blanket in her arms, as one would do with a tiny infant. I asked her how old the child was and she said "six years". I said, "You mean six months?" "No, six years." I could only give her money to take the baby to the hospital in Merida. I doubt the baby lived another year. I normally used medications I was familiar with rather than those I had to look up. Antibiotics are not effective against viruses but my own experience is that I usually have a secondary, bacterial infection. If I can defeat one, I have a better chance with the other. Especially for those who are grown, I've found lomotil (also available in Mexico without a prescription) extremely effective against the flux. Once I came down with the flux and a bit of temperature. I took some lomotil pills surrounded by neomyicin and if I recall correctly, slept, waking only for the bathroom for 3 days. When that period was over, I felt great. Sleep has such great curative powers. When patients were seen, it was quite impossible to achieve any level of confidentiality. There was always more of a number of them in queue. I believe some folk just needed a little TLC. Over the years however, I've treated hundreds of people there. All have either gotten better or showed no signs of having gotten worse. I will admit nevertheless, that my success may be more of a testimony for placebo than skill. The government would later occasionally send in a nurse but all such programs were short lived. The Director of the Red Cross in Merida and an administrative doctor in Oxkutzcab tried to get doctors interested in going to Yaxachen, but to no avail. It was considered too far away with too much wasted time.

Another child was brought to me that had large hump on the small of the back, with a hole in it. I had never seen spinal bifida but I figured this was serious. We gave her money to take the child, Wilson de Xul, immediately to Merida. She did so, and I made arrangements for paying for the operation such children must have to survive. I was given a discount on all operations. Lina worked matters out so I later paid $400 for a $3,000 operation. The boy was always curious to me. He was blonde headed and where did the name "Wilson" come from? It sounded as if he was born in Xul, not in Yaxachen. None of that mattered other than my curiosity. I have wondered since if he might have been the child of the New Yorker who originally wrote me about Yaxachen. I learned in time that the operation was a success.

Myself and Wilson de Xul, the boy born with spina bifida.

Wilson became the pet of the hospital staff. I was not to see him for some years later, for his family moved to Oxkutzcab, probably to be closer to medical care. When I saw him he had become a teen and while he walked with a limp, he got around fine. He asked me for bicycle money, which I gave him. I found out much later that spinal bifida and other birth defects are the result of insufficient folic acid in the diet during early pregnancy. So for want of some green leafy vegetables or pills that one can get anywhere for a few cents each, Wilson came near to dying and walked with a limp all his life. When our beans ran low we would drive to Oxkutzcab and return with more plus many crates of fresh fruit. I wondered, but never got around to asking why they did not grow oranges in the village. I finally did buy them a few orange trees. I have found not sweeter oranges in the world than Yucatan's and no better mangos.

Over the years, there have been numerous serious medical conditions in the village and there were few old people there. They just did not live too long under such conditions.

Before we had worked many days on the road, medical clinic, food dispensary, and garden, I went into Merida to see what they offered in the way of a pump. The water level was three hundred feet beneath the surface at the end of the four-foot diameter open pit well. With no electricity to lift water, it would require a powerful gasoline pump. Lina again came to our aid saving us much time and looking. The name of the company was Rincon and they sold pumps that could do the job.

What the pump company owner showed us in his brochure looked like an oil field pump with a long armature that went up and down, run by a gasoline motor. When asked about problems with the pump he said, pointing to the pump, "This is not your problem; this is your problem (pointing to the gasoline engine)." He was honest and correct. The real shocker was the price - $2,750. It supposedly included installation. I paid for the pump but that called for a drastic, immediate revision of our plan. We agreed the ladies and I would return to the states immediately, wherein I would raise minimal funds needed to support the small group left behind to make sure the pump got installed and worked properly. Three volunteers wanted to stay, 2 wanted to leave (the ladies) and I and another agreed to do whatever would benefit the project. Also, the road was months from being finished. So I left them all the funds I could, except what we needed to get home. I hated to leave the remaining volunteers with no vehicle other than the occasional government or merchant truck coming by. After all, the village was not a place you could call 911 or if you were in a cave 300 feet below that a helicopter could be sent to extract you. I left the group with over $250.00 cash and several weeks of food.

Lina arranged for the men to be housed cheaper in a warehouse when they had to be in Merida, and for a neighborhood woman to cook their meals while there. I sent the money as needed and anxiously awaited the report. I had been in the village for one month. The men stayed there for a total of six months, not only overseeing the pump (which to our chagrin cost $300 more than quoted), but overseeing the roadwork as well. When the money was gone for hiring road workers, the crew, and Lena, convinced the Mexican government to pay the village men, in kind, for working on the road. They were given daily food.

When the pump was installed and began shooting water into the holding tank, there was great jubilation. The water that came out was clean, without the usual sediment. It worked perfectly and a line was rigged up to fill tanks for nearby settlements. Before long, I had the water tested and it was pronounced good, only polluted by vessels they carried it in. A procedure was developed whereby those getting water from the well would pay 20 centavos. This, we thought, would produce a fund for pump repair when necessary. Unfortunately, too many didn't ever have the 20 centavos so the plan collapsed. I can't recall whether that plan was my brainstorm or Dad's. We both enjoyed flight of fancy. Some ideas came into fruition and some of our ideas were merely wish list items of things we'd have done if we had the time and resources. Never again would they have to use the giant spool. Years later, when it became obvious that the spool days were over, they gave it to me as a rather large memento. I had the base dug up and placed it in my pick up. I was stopped by Federales with automatic weapons in Central Mexico, and was asked where I was taking it. It has a seamless metal ring around the top that was bent. I pointed to the bend and said, "See that? I'm taking it into a mechanic to straighten." They sent me on my way. God knows what they were looking for. I was just a small target of opportunity. I took it home, disassembled, treated, reassembled, and it stands now in my valley as a reminder of how hard life can be.

So when the remainder of my original crew left, the pump was providing good water for the whole village and they had a road you could drive down at speeds up to twenty miles per hour, the whole nine and one half mile length.

The Mayor, Senor Lawreano by the pump I bought for the village.

The road the villagers, crew and I built. It goes straight to the capital and eventually becomes a paved road, as it merges into the capital.

The plan underwent major changes, but the mission was accomplished. God bless those volunteers wherever they are.

I had planned that the first would be my last trip to Yaxachen, but it was not to be. As I had left, Santiago, a tall, middle age man who played the guitar and sang, serenaded us. And he told me, "We will be working in the fields, think of you, and sigh." I had thought of myself as fairly immune to flattery, but that impressed me. Was it his demeanor or the words he chose? I do not know. But the following year, I returned to make sure things were o.k. I returned twice that year and for many years thereafter. The road and the pump were basic necessary steps. And while the road better linked them to markets and services, it did not alone solve all of their problems.

I kept returning because I did not know of a place on earth where I was more needed. I kept returning because we had wonderful rapport and they presented themselves, and their problems, as clay to be molded by me. I kept returning because I had nothing else as important to do. I kept returning because I did not want to spend my life at country clubs, in front of the television, or just being pampered. I kept returning because my philosophy is that no one should have dozens of shoes while some have none. I kept returning because it was a world where a man that was not handy could fix things. I have said many times to friends, "When I am in the village and they set a table in the yard with folding chairs, and make me and my companions chicken soup with a large stack of corn tortillas, well, it does not get any better than that for me." They have so little to offer that when they offer it, it fuses my soul to theirs. I have had old women and even men, grab my hand and kiss it. How then shall I tell them to kiss off?

Over the years, I have taken many professionals and just the curious. I never turned anyone down. It allowed them to truly see how radically different much of the world lives, and it allowed me to take so many gifts to villagers. Over the years, I've taken enough books in Spanish to form a small library. These would include a set of encyclopedias, books on agriculture, first aid, and vitamins. I've taken recreational equipment for volleyball and baseball, and after receiving such the men would often spend their idle time on those sports. Fairly quickly, the village went from one of only necessary activity, to one more filled with life.

CHAPTER 9

The events I now tell you about have lost their chronological place in line. I cannot remember their year and so I batch them for the telling. And besides, what can be more boring than giving dates?

One clinic morning, an elderly man came complaining of phenomenon connected to a head injury. He mentioned that he was in a tree, fell, and landed on his head. Since that time, occasionally he would hear thunder but would go outside, look up, and see nothing but clear, blue sky. Also, he would be walking and suddenly freeze in place in whatever position he was in. He was laughing about his symptoms and got us to laughing too. I told him it sounded as if he had incurred some brain damage. I told him if he wished, we could take a machete, open his skull, take out his brain and see if we could figure out what was wrong. I took my finger and drew a line about five inches down my own skull to show him the size of the incision we would have to make. He smiled and said, "O.k." Then, of course, still laughing, I explained we could not do that and gave him money to go the city for an x-ray.

A man in his thirties came to clinic and showed what appeared to be a bad case of gonorrhea. I am told gonorrhea eventually runs its course in about a year but, when it does, your reproductive organs are ruined. This is to say nothing of the agony. I mentioned my diagnosis and suggested he stay away from the putas (prostitutes) in Oxkutzcab. There, prostitutes would come, I am told, during festivals. He did not deny the diagnosis, but denied it was caused by a woman in the city. He said it came upon him when he was working on the road and bent in an awkward position, demonstrating it for us. I have heard of gonorrhea being blamed on the toilet seat and many other extraneous factors, but that was a new one on me. I gave him sufficient antibiotics for both himself and his wife.

Over the years I have taken three doctors to the village, two nurses, a pharmacist, and lab tech, and always allowed them to dispense the medication during the period they were there. I have never represented myself as a doctor or medico, only someone with medicine. But I quickly learned I knew first aid and far more about medicine than the villagers did. I sometimes referred to the Physicians Desk Reference and the Merck Manual, and I tried to err on the side of caution if anything. I took the same medicine when I came down with the same ailments, and generally considered myself infinitely superior to ancient practitioners. Of course, I did lots of referring and tried not to get too cute, too quick. The problem use of the Merck Manuel, particularly to the layman and one without benefit of lab tests, is that too many diseases have the same symptoms.

The one time I thought I had gone too far was when I saw who was probably the oldest woman in the village. She was in pain and I had given her a pain pill. Her son brought her back shortly thereafter, and described symptoms that I thought might be cardiac distress. I was nervous. My first reaction was to explain to him it could not be the pain pill, and I swallowed one myself to demonstrate their benigness. Right after I had done so, the old lady began to belch. She must have burped twenty times in a row. Then she felt fine. I am guessing that the pill, without food, might have upset her stomach. She did not ask for another pill and I did not offer. I felt a bit of stomach upset myself after that incident.

On more than one occasion, I found a nurse more useful than a physician. I believe they were bolder in their treatment, whereupon the doctor was used to being backed by his lab tests, screenings, etc. and had concerns about the obscure and unlikely, but possible, disorders and ramifications. They carried baggage of fear of lawsuits and malpractice that the nurses brushed off under those circumstances. Too, the doctors would sometimes give instructions in preciseness that were hard to remember or follow. Or perhaps the instructions were just too expensive to follow. A man came to clinic when I had a nurse who looked as though his hand had been bitten by a large carnivore. It was badly swollen and infected. The nurse cleaned the wound, wrapped his hand and gave him antibiotics. There was no talk of finding the animal to have it quarantined, rabies shots, or x-rays. None of that would have made any sense to the man. He went on his way practically treated and feeling better. There was little talk of getting the Mexican government's permission for a medical practice, which would have been an arduous labor, ending in frustration. Nor was there much talk of making arrangements to work under the license of a practicing Mexican doctor. We would fly in, do what we could quietly, and leave quickly on most trips.

I always dreamed of driving into isolated villages in Mexico's mountains, in my old pickup, with a chest of medicines trading treatment for lunch. There are so many spots that have never seen a doctor or nurse, and I am sure they would be the better for it. Yet, if such spots are remote from medical facilities, they are also remote from mechanics and parts houses. I am a bit old to fancy walking out of the mountains on a fifty-mile trek. Too, people of such areas tend to be xenophobic, fearful and suspicious of strangers. And, they are as lacking in law officers as anything else.

My own village has no police though they have been known to rent one for special occasions. They usually knew when I would be coming for the weekend because Jorge would get on the radio and inform them. My friends and I were amazed on one trip when we were stopped just at the edge of town. Hanging high was a sign in Spanish that said, "Welcome to Villa Linda de Yaxachen." I had previously asked if they would mind if we named the road to Yaxachen "Calle Linda" in honor of my wife who had supported my efforts on their behalf over the years. They had done much more, and had renamed the village. I do not believe the name stuck year in and out because it was a mouthful. Many people liked the name however, and Jorge, who later became a skilled carpenter, gave me a duplicate sign for my keeping.

*The ceremony renaming the town from Yaxachen to
Villa Linda de Yaxachen in honor of my wife.*

Too, airports, towns, and streets are always undergoing renaming. But then and there, I stood in Villa Linda de Yaxachen. Even more stunning were the pretty young women, freshly scrubbed and in their best Huipeles (white dresses with square necks surrounded by embroidered flowers) who came to receive us. There was a woman on each arm to escort us to the square. I know that must have been awkward for them as unaccustomed as they were to touching strange males. The entire village had gathered. In the center of the plaza was a multilayered cake made by Feficiano, the baker. They had even hired a uniformed policeman, and had a city stamp with the new name on it. Photos were taken and I was led to a large red ribbon to cut, inaugurating the town. I was a little embarrassed but very grateful.

After I had worked in the village for several years off and on, they decided to introduce me to some of their personal attractions. On the road to which I now call Calle Linda, there was a turn off leading to a large, poor, private ranch. The road to the ranch is now mainly paved because it leads to a set of ruins they call Kiwic. A few villagers and I went there in a heavy-duty truck that was in town for the day. Usually the few local villagers would take bicycles since the ruins stand some three miles off the road. The most significant thing about the ruins of Kiwic is that they are totally unreconstructed. While the jungle has done its damage since about 800 A.D., there is one building, perhaps eighty feet long, which is perfectly intact. There is another, single temple face, that has a haunting allure, and there are numerous Tells. To the side is a large bat cave with a cathedral ceiling. There are natural huge stone steps allowing easy access to the bottom, but help is needed to get out. One cannot help but wonder what noble(s) lies buried underneath the temple building floors awaiting proper excavation.

Approximately two miles from the village in another direction, lies the Grotto of Yaxachen. Villagers spoke of a stone lady at the bottom and tell of ancient times when men would have to descend to the bottom of it for scarce water. They knew I wanted to go to the bottom so when they heard by radio I was coming, they built a ladder two hundred and fifty feet long for me to descend. The ladder was built of jungle saplings and was built in sections since the descent is not always straight down.

I came to the natural opening, which may have been five feet in diameter. I picked up a few pebbles and threw them in and they disappeared into inky blackness. But, flashlight in hand and testing the strength of the ladder rungs, I began the descent. I would go perhaps twenty feet and would find a ledge with the next section of the ladder off to the side.

To my annoyance, it looked like half a dozen villagers were following me, and my sixty-five year old dad with them. Eventually, I reached the bottom where there were pools of standing water - a long climb for very little. The "stone lady" was a wall rock formation that one had to use a lot of imagination to see a lady in it. It was rather like the salt column that is pointed at as Lot's wife beside the Dead Sea.

For a brief, concerned moment, one of the current volunteers got lost in a lateral cave at the bottom. No sound penetrated that rock. He had not gone far and managed his own way back.

The assent involved some of the ladder rungs busting loose and everyone seemed glad to see the light above.

After working in the village for yet more years, I was shown a well-concealed single, intact temple. I asked some of the men whether they had ever considered digging and they said, "No. The man from the government knows where the buildings are, and he comes around and inspects. He may not come for a year but when he comes, if the ground has been disturbed, he asks questions. And they have ways of getting answers." I will go to my grave with the location of that temple.

The entire area of Villa Linda is an archeological zone. Yucatan has so very many ruins with so little funds to excavate.

The costly pump in the Villa Linda lasted eighteen years, with some occasional repairs to the gasoline motor running it. It was beautiful to see the villagers go to one of the many taps along the bottom of the tank and obtain clean water. The water was sweet and clean but the metal carrying cans were often rusty and dirty. Little girls were hauling two five-gallon cans of water (just over eighty pounds of water) using a shoulder yoke. I decided to chlorinate the holding tank but I was unable to effectively judge the amount of water in the tank. I poured in an entire gallon of Clorox. The water coming out smelled like a hundred swimming pools back to back. They pumped water through for a few hours before it had the very slight chlorine smell that I was aiming for. In concert with this, I lined up every available member of the village and gave them a spoon of worm medicine. My technique may have been crude, but for some time thereafter, there was less diarrhea and fewer parasites.

Just as the pump, after eighteen years, had breathed its last, the government put electricity into Villa Linda. At that point, I bought them a submersible pump, which was far cheaper and more efficient. I am convinced the timing was God engineered. A local Dutch minister installed the pump for them and has installed several since.

Somewhere along the line we were told that Lina had cancer and she soon died. At the time, we were so heavily engrossed in the work we had time only for a silent moment. We were as a hive of bees intent on building the hive - so intent, that nothing mattered but that the hive is built. And when even a key worker like her fell to an enemy, we just pressed forward. But, over the years, in quiet moments, I pray for the repose of her soul and I hurt from the wound.

After I had worked in the village more than twenty years, I encountered another case of spinal bifida in a little girl named Delmi. I was emboldened, after the success of Wilson's operation for the same malady, and quickly arranged an operation for her. The operation saved her life but she would never walk. I have wondered a thousand times if I did her a favor. Growing up in a village so primitive was difficult enough without that disability. In the beginning, I gave her a wheel chair, which was so huge for such a tiny girl. And the path to school was often rocky. Then, I was given two tricycles that were hand operated. In time, she outgrew these, even with small, atrophied legs. In the year 2005, I got a bargain on an electric scooter. I had asked her family the year before if they wanted one for her since it would not last forever, and wondered if, having once had one, she would not be worse off. Nevertheless, her family wanted it. So, I bought it and drove the seventeen hundred miles to deliver it. They seemed very pleased.

Over the years, I have taken the villagers tons of donated clothing, treadle sewing machines, and bicycles bought in Merida and whatever I took, they put to good use. Oddly, blankets were highly prized because the temperatures in the nights of December and January can get into the high forties. Always I took medicines, tools, toys, and even fireworks. The children loved 'sparklers'. Instead of running about holding the cold end, they would toss them high in the air and rush to retrieve them, repeating the process.

Having criticized the Mexican government, it would be unfair not to offer praise where due. It showed flexibility absent in our own government. When the government agreed to pay the road workers in food after my money ran out, they showed that compassion had greater value than rules. Too, once when I ran out of gasoline at a military checkpoint, a Major sent one of his men to get me gasoline, and refused a tip. I was awed. I cannot picture our own military having the flexibility to so assist a Mexican out wandering around the U.S. I can only salute the Mexican spirit that overrides regulations and procedures for the greater good.

Among the memories is the day we saw heavy laden rain clouds coming toward the village. To beat the rains, having given everything away, we leaped into the truck and raced toward Xul. We had left too late, and a great deluge ensued. I hit a deep puddle going fast and the rain shot up under the hood. The motor died and would not restart, so we walked the remainder of the way to Xul, perhaps four miles. Once there, darkness had set in, so we went into one of the vacant buildings on the square, which had once served as the school. We stretched out on the dirt floor and, after sleeping for a while, I awoke noticing some movement by my face. I knew that sometimes children of Yucatan had kept tarantulas as pets, teaching them to jump. I also knew that tarantulas are harmless, with a sting less than a bee. However, they are simply so creepy looking, I reached for my flashlight and found myself eye to eye with a large frog. I did not know who was more startled – him or me. At daybreak, we managed to get aboard a truck going our way and went to a mechanico in Oxkutzcab. He had us buy a few parts and said he would buy back any he did not need, driving us back to our abandoned truck. He did his quick magic, the truck started, and he received a round of applause. He looked at us incredulously as if to say, "Well what did you expect?" It all cost very little.

Over Christmas, when I arrived in the village, I had been determined to cook Christmas dinner for the village. I had gone by the supermarket in Merida buying potatoes, carrots, onions, tomato sauce and a large church of beef. By that time, I had mastered getting to the village in just a few hours. The large, institutional cooking pot I had brought on the first trip had long since disappeared as all gifts did. I did have a large laundry type pot. I quickly cut the beef into small slices, had folks start a fire and bring the water. Perhaps and hour or two later, I noted that the pan was too thin. I had not stirred enough, and lots of the beef was stuck to the bottom. Well, I did not exactly get my training in cooking at the Escoffier in Paris, so it was something of a minor failure. Nevertheless, they ate it and the men pried the meat off the bottom and wolfed it as well.

One of the unsolved mysteries was how to disperse the goods in a really fair manner. I tried dispersing some myself, giving a large portion to the Commissario to disperse, or giving it to the churches to distribute. I never heard complaints from the people, but I always wondered if I was doing it right. I did hear Commissario Laureano once chastise someone saying, "That is for the poor." As if everyone there was not pitifully poor. On one of my last trips, I decided to leave it to chance. I brought a BINGO game and the prizes were things like a loaded tool chest, five pounds of sugar and flour, a blanket, etc. It took very few moments for them to learn the game and then, a good time was had by all. I would holler at the children in Spanish, "Que es mas importante, mi vida o BINGO?" (What is more important, my life or BINGO?) They would shout, "BINGO," followed by much laughter.

One year, a young friend and I brought a group of optometrists from the University of Houston School of Optometry. They brought about three hundred sets of eyeglasses that had been 'neutralized' and put those with visual difficulties through a multi-staged eye exam. They outfitted about seventy-five people with eyeglasses and left behind the other sets so the villagers could sift and lift after we left. In the beginning years, I always stayed nights. But as the trips became more routine, and my skill at dispersing got better, I would often just stay a few hours, long enough to unload and give away.

With the coming of readily available water, there for just turning the tap, they became more interested in having some animals. Once, a man came with a truckload of chickens at one and two dollars apiece. I bought the truckload. The villagers saw to the division.

I had tried again through a doctor connected to the Red Cross to get medical students to go to the village on tour. I had even paid down on the enterprise. The doctor could not however, find sufficient interest. The location was too remote and the facilities too primitive I suppose. He refunded.

For many years, I just loved shopping for the people of Villa Linda de Yaxachen while in the U.S. Primarily, shopping in a foreign country is labor intensive. There are areas in the central business district where cars cannot be driven, and all you need is rarely in one place. Therefore, it entails long, hot walks on very crowded streets. And while basic staples are cheaper there, all technology is more expensive whether you are talking about a radio or appliances. In the U.S., I could leisurely stroll the aisles, thinking about things that would amuse, awe, or instruct the villagers. At a garage sale, I bought the aforementioned Spanish encyclopedias and have taken first aid books in Spanish which they read haltingly. They also always enjoyed receiving Bibles in Spanish. In the early, pre-electric days, flashlights and batteries were always a premium item. Later, blankets to protect against the winter nights, and cooking oil rose in value.

I kept a standing invitation for anyone to go with me, and dozens did over the years. Some came mainly out of curiosity; some wanted to be of help. But whatever their reason, I would consistently ask that they fit all personal luggage into a flight bag so that I could have their check-in baggage allowance. Donations may be harder to come by than you anticipate. But almost everyone is willing to give clothing and villagers can always use warm weather clothing. Linda would sew oversized blue jean duffle bags or I would buy some at the army surplus and stuff them with items for the villagers just beneath a thin layer of my own clothes. I was almost never checked and the few times I was, they appeared mainly to be looking either for contraband or high prized items. In my amateur smuggling efforts, I was always prepared to pay a fine if necessary. I have always been very reluctant however, to pay bribes. As such, a corrupt system is fed and it makes matters worse for those who come after you. Once, my dad, a friend, and I were parked at the curb in Oxkutzcab, and were rear-ended by a drunken motor scooter driver. The accident knocked him out. I pulled him from the street and, as he came to, asked if he wanted us to take him to the doctor. Three times I asked and three times he said, "No." So we started driving away when a ragged non-uniform policeman pulled along side with instructions to follow him to the police station. At the station, the officer in charge wanted $10 to get the man an x-ray. I had no problem on humanitarian grounds, forking over the $10. But it seemed to me that such action might be looked upon as an admission of guilt so I refused. The police officer got loud and so did I. My friend went back to the cells and told me, "Ray, I think we better pay, I just had a look at the cells and they have a dirt floor and one all purpose bucket." I exclaimed, "I am not paying anything, we did not do anything wrong." After perhaps fifteen minutes of arguing, the policeman told us to get out and be on our way.

Always, I would take very large stacks of one-dollar bills. They could easily get those changed into pesos at the bank in Oxkutzcab. Larger bills were a problem and I could never get the Casa de Cambios (change house) to give me sufficient small pesos notes. The bank in Yucatan was always questioning where the people got so many U.S. ones, yet never created a disturbance over it. Oddly, even today, in the country regions of Mexico, they do not accept dollars that have a little corner torn off or other imperfections such as writing on them. Or, they want to give you a percentage of its value. So before I would go to Mexico, I would check each dollar to make sure it was whole and not badly marred.

Sunday in the village, I always tried to attend church. While I had no idea what they were talking about other than picking up every eighth word, I thought it good modeling to go. The churches were mainly well attended by the women. The men seemed to particularly forgo worship as conditions improved in the village.

It was not always possible to tie the giving of money to work. Sometimes the people asking simply needed small amounts quickly for emergency purposes. I disregarded text book admonitions about the outright giving of money being degrading. If you give it in love, they accept it in love.

One year I got the macabre idea after listening to some talk of the local cemetery and the shallow graves that I'd like to have a skull to take home as a deeply personal reminder of the village and of the mortality of us all. They said they had done some cleaning of the cemetery but had no hesitancy in agreeing to my request. They took me to the village cemetery where they showed me a small stone sarcophagus. We rolled back the stone lid and there, sitting on the ground, were 2 full human skulls without a body. I don't know why. As I reached for one I felt like a character in a Rudyard Kipling story who was reaching for a ruby that was guarded by a cobra. I went to lift the skull only to find that the tropics and oxidation had done their work. It crumbled to dust in my hand. I gave up the idea and I certainly did not want to do anything to disrespect the dead.

In all the time spent in the village over the years, other than correcting man imposed animal discomforts, I only had to be stern with one person. He was drunk. I'd never seen a villager drink before and I guessed that he was returning from a festival in Oxkutzcab. He was getting rough with his wife and I yelled, "No, no". He turned around and grumbled something at me but he quit his spouse abuse. I believe in self-determination but all principles have at least one boundary, and I make no apologies to anyone for defending the weak. Yet the village has no jail and I've never seen a fight there. I can assume that social structure keeps things pretty well intact.

CONCLUSION OF YUCATAN

Through the years I have seen many changes in the village, and the coming of electricity probably topped them all. Houses have branched out along the road. The streets have become paved by the government which brought in more heavy equipment than anyone had seen in the state, and made a new road atop the road we had made, straightening the errors and smoothing and widening. Whereas my road permitted speeds of approximately twenty miles per hour, now the road allows for up to sixty miles per hour. The government put in a basketball court where the young men play under court lights throughout the night. There are more chickens and pigs than ever before. Now there is a Catholic Church in town in addition to two Presbyterian Churches. On my last trip, I noticed two houses under construction that would not look out of the place in blue collar suburban America. Some of the young men have jobs in Oxkutzcab as pedal taxi drivers, some as laborers elsewhere. A few people from Villa Linda de Yaxachen even migrate to the U.S. working as fruit pickers. There is considerable contact with the outside world today. When my road had been finished, the owner of a private bus company began daily service to the village. The bus would come in the night, stay, and leave the next morning. Unfortunately, the people mainly used free transportation when it was available, and the bus owner, in a huff, said he would be canceling the service since they did not patronize it well. While this was all understandable, it was regrettable since guaranteed daily service would give them a way to visit a doctor in case of dire need.

Mainly, the village has an optimism it formerly lacked, along with a much-elevated level of activity rather than passively waiting to die.

The village will always be poor, for they have long needed someone with different skills than I have developed. They need someone who can help them form a credit union or committees for micro-loans. They need assistance to help them collectively sell their crops at better prices. They need someone who understands business and the mechanics of their local system. Once I considered sending a villager to a trade school but what would keep him, upon graduating, from moving to the city to improve his lot in life. I could not blame him, but wherein would the village profit?

On my last trip in 2005, there was only one man living of the original adults I had begun to work with. He is Feliciano, originally the storeowner, corn grinder, and baker. My dear friend Feliciano, so straight and handsome in olden days, is now bowed and thin. He still musters a smile though both he and I know tomorrow does not belong to us. But that is okay. I know that I had purpose, and that the village will continue with someone building on my efforts. When I had been called on to give a speech, I would in essence tell them, "While I may have said, 'Action,

Camera', it was God who directed, and the wonderful people of Villa Linda de Yaxachen who played their parts so successfully on life's stage. Viva Villa Linda de Yaxachen!"

They now have a good 9.5-mile road connecting them to the outer world along with electricity and a water pump, all they dreamed of before 1971. While a village now stands there, it is not my village anymore. The men I worked with and for have gone to God. And it is I who sigh when recollection of those times return. And the village has grown from the original 400 to 1200 at last count. A nurse, who was a part of the group I once took, gave a lecture on birth control. It was well attended but mainly by the men.

My chief regret is that I did not have the language skills and the time to get to know villagers on a more personal level. I found them among the sweetest people on earth. They were consistently quiet, polite, and often eloquent of speech. There is a shyness between genders and while the separation never reaches the level of Moslem countries, a wall is there nevertheless.

Jorge has consistently made himself available to me for a village trip whenever I have gone to Yucatan. In a recent year I had taken one of the hand-operated tricycles on a cruise that docked briefly at Cozumel. Jorge met the cruise and took the tricycle to deliver it to the village. I have steadfastly raised his salary and finally paid him $50.00 for a day trip rather than the $5.00 when he started. For many years I have called him brother and when my last parent died, I bought him a Honda motor scooter to replace his worn out Mexican scooter. This, I explained, was his cut of my mother's will.

Some years back the villagers built me a house on the outskirts of town, dedicated to the Cryer Foundation. But I used it so little they finally asked if they could use it for other purposes which I thought was a far better idea. They finally got one television for the whole village. It had a very tall antenna and receives poor reception. There are now two flush toilets in the village. The Mexican pipes are not able, however, to handle toilet paper, which must be placed in a can beside the toilet. There are even 2 showers, but the water is cold leaving one feeling as though he needs another shower 10 minutes later in the tropical heat. Three men in the village serve as barbers, and as of 2003 you could get a haircut and shave for 50 cents.

I got a shave for half that amount while sitting on a folding chair in the barber's yard. The government came and put in playground equipment on the square, including the basketball court.

Over the years I and those interested in going to the village, have gotten there usually by renting a car in Merida after flying into Yucatan. However, we have also gone in the back of a fruit truck that we paid to deliver us and some of its cargo. Once friends and I even went from Merida to Oxkutzcab by train (no longer running) that was perhaps the slowest service I've ever experienced. In or around trade centers there are always vehicles going your way or willing to do so for a nominal fee. On one occasion we even hired a taxi in Merida to take us the 90 miles to the village. The road we had built was finished so the cab driver could deliver us without damage to his vehicle. Yet when we arrived and the people came out to meet us the driver had a stunned look on his face. It seemed to say, "I can't believe I've driven you to the end of the world, are you going to leave me alone here?" It was so comical I could not suppress a laugh. We did give him a generous tip if that counted for anything. A legally blind friend held an Easter Egg hunt with candy eggs in the village. It is hard to hide eggs with a large crowd of children looking on. But in a place where it is difficult to even go to the bathroom unaccompanied, one might have expected that.

Items I have always found useful in villages are as follows:

> Salt (two liters of water, a half cup of sugar, and
> a teaspoon of salt have probably save more lives
> then antibiotics due to people otherwise dying of
> dehydration from the flux)
> Sugar
> Cooking oil
> Antibiotics (over the counter in Mexico)
> Vitamins
> Triple antibiotic ointment
> Soap (bar and detergent)
> Bibles in their language
> Aspirin
> Dried foods (fruit, cereal, noodles, rice, beans)
> Clorox (for water purification)

Oral thermometer
Powdered milk
Paper cups for dispensing pills
A couple of pots and pans
Flux (diarrhea) medicine
Plastic canteens for water
Paper and pencils
Army surplus portable shower
Shoes
Glasses for reading
Hydrogen Peroxide (for cleaning wounds)
Bandages
A Merck Manual
First-aid manual

CHAPTER 10

HAITI

Having accomplished the major work in Yucatan to my satisfaction, I was feeling cocky, at least compared to pre-Yucatan. I wonder what differences I would encounter in another culture, or if the lessons I'd learned were universal. I wanted to check it out with different people in a different place.

I cannot recall when I did not want to go to Haiti. A little Maryland sized country discovered by Columbus on his first trip to the new world in 1492 sounded incredibly exotic. The successful slave revolt against the French had made it the second republic in the Western Hemisphere, just behind the United States. I had seen a few snapshots of the country and had gotten some titillating tidbits from movies. I imagined it to be a lush land with jungle, fruit, plantations, and happy people. That may have been Haiti 100 years ago, I do not know. Alas, like most of the Caribbean, it has nothing to offer the world but tourist facilities.

I had shelved my dreams of going to Haiti for decades. And what if it wasn't as I'd fantasized? Life is not having a perfect plan; often it is making a bad plan work.

I have come to believe somewhat in omens. When I saw an article in *Time Magazine* entitled, "Haiti: Island of Hunger", I figured it was the kind of place I sought, because if the inhabitants had in abundance, they would neither want nor need me. When I found that U.N. statistics listed it as the fourth poorest country in the world, the matter was settled. Additionally, a report from the Agency for International Development stated, "The United Nations has devised a list of the world's 26 least developed countries. Haiti is the only Western Hemisphere country included in the list". Prevalent diseases included influenza, gastio-intestinal disorder, hookworm, TB, pellagra, scurvy, malaria, polio, typhoid fever, and scabies. It sounded like a place where I could have a positive impact regardless of what errors I made.

I met with a group of Academicians at UTMB explaining my intent. They were roughly familiar with my work in Yucatan, and some expressed a desire to accompany me. I have always found academicians self involved, shallow in their commitments, and easily derailed, however, an anthropologist with lots of foreign field experience agreed to go and actually did so.

I had some reservations about going with a lone female, but she turned out to be a tough, yet very pleasant person, and I was glad to have company. Going alone involved additional risks, and besides, two heads are usually better.

Once the target country was selected and I had committed, I read everything I could about Haiti, including Graham Green's horrific novel, "The Comedians". The shocking stories of Haiti under Francoise Duvalier had abated with his death, and everyone hoped Jean-Claude Duvalier, "Baby Doc" would be a healing balm to the wound of Papa Doc. When Pappa Doc had been "elected", voters were told they could vote as many times as they liked during the election as long as their ballet bore the name of Francoise Duvalier (Pappa Doc). He was originally elected for 6 years but then later became "President for life". Murder of all suspected opponents became a vital Presidential pastime. But by the time I would arrive, Pappa Doc had been deceased a few years. The Macoute Tonton were still there but somewhat hunkered down.

My search for information on Haiti was less than satisfying. I could find only one person who had ever been there, and her trip was a luxury ship stopover 15 years before. Too, this elderly woman had only seen the area around the dock where the ship moored. If a country has nothing to offer, they at least spruce up the area at dockside with picturesque shops and stands. And a 4-6 hour stopover makes penetration of the interior difficult. Also, most ocean liners had stopped making call there years before. Cruise patrons want to see gayety, not misery. They are there to forget their problems, not take on those of others.

The "Area Handbook of Haiti", found at the U.S. Government printing office, yielded the most data. However, in impoverished third world countries, I am suspect of any figures no matter who collected them. I had read "Transaction" Magazine about a census in Calcutta. It gave estimates of people living on the street of between 50,000 and 2 million. That is quite a range of guessing. A brief trip to Calcutta once, had revealed the difficulty in trying to gather accurate information. An 82-page report on Haiti by A.I.D. seemed of little use for my purposes. It was filled with generalized concepts, large production fluctuations, world prices, transportation deficits, and talk of the need to develop local leadership. I found myself wishing it had been written by a farmer rather than an academic. It did tell some interesting estimates, for example, that the literacy of the Haitian population was between 20-30%. Rural literacy was less than 5%. While it was short on answers and admitted many uncertainties, it pointed directly at some of the problems. One big problem was the "evident lack of concern of the urban elite . . . for the rural population". The per capita income estimate was less than $50.00 per year. Yet another 13 page report from USAID of September 1975 said the "per capita, is roughly $140.00 per year, the lowest in the Western Hemisphere." Also, that "population density is 460 persons per square mile, one of the highest in the Western Hemisphere". Whatever the true figure of per capita income, it was obviously a grim one. It was apparent from the reports also that erosion, exploding population, and poor infrastructure were prime difficulties. There was much written of grant, programs and studies, but I saw nothing other than some notable road improvements completed just before my second trip to Haiti. But even if all the plans worked it would still leave so many Haitians unserved. And I became a living witness that the project 033 "Malaria Eradication" fell short of its goal. The report indicated CARE was an acronym for Cooperative for American Relief Everywhere. Also that a continuing drought in NW Haiti "has wiped out the spring/summer planting of crops resulting in severe hardship and food scarcity". Small farm units of 10 acres in size accounted for 75% of farmland. Produce taken to market would be taxed arbitrarily by private entities with much of the money never going to the government.

In short, Haiti had, and has, every kind of problem one can imagine. Life expectancy in Haiti was 48 years. All this, I was going into.

The material on Haiti indicated that their inheritance laws were fashioned under French law. If a man who had 8 sons in Haiti died, his land was divided equally into 8 parts. Thus, land parcels become smaller and smaller, negating the use of sizable farm equipment. Finally, lawyers got 1/5 of the land upon arranging the transfer. This in a country where 2/3 of the land is unsuitable for farming.

I learned additionally, that Haiti was only about 1/3 of the isle of Hispaniola. Mountains, which separate Haiti from the Dominican Republic, block the moister laden clouds, leaving the Northwest Department of Haiti in a frequent state of drought. It was the Northwest that inspired the "Time" article, and caused that Department to be labeled "The area of Famine." Prior to our arrival, it had not rained there for eight months. I had always assumed that if you dug deep enough you'd hit sweet water. That was certainly an error. There are many areas of the world without a water table (the point at which the ground is totally saturated with water). Some areas have not aquifers, but tiny pockets of below ground water that you may hit or miss while digging. Below a certain level, water is rarely found so one could dig indefinitely and never hit water. On costal areas, and islands, dryness results in salt-water encroachment. Unless you have sufficient rainfall to keep the salt water at bay, it seeps into dry pockets everywhere. Salt-water encroachment can occur as far as 75 miles inland. Places like the island of Galveston, Texas, receive their water from inland. You can go just beyond the first set of sand dunes, dig shallow, and find the lighter, brackish water floating on top of the salt water. However, there is not enough to sustain a sizable group of people. I was undeterred by this information. I knew there were places in this world where people should not live, at least not many. But they did live in the Northwest by some means, and I wanted to improve those means.

I read that voodoo was a major phenomenon in Haiti, but I thought that was more Hollywood hype than reality. I was to later find the opposite. Everyone in Haiti, with the exception of a small handful of foreigners, believed very strongly in voodoo.

The literature I read in Haiti, aside from government books, tended to glamorize the accomplishments of the country. Alexander Dumas, the prolific author of "The Count of Monte Cristo", "The Three Musketeers", and well over 100 other stories, had been the grandson of a Haitian slave. Haiti was the first black republic in the Western Hemisphere. It had been a rich colony for France and a supplier of huge amounts of fruit for the U.S. Yet everyone seemed to take from Haiti while no one put much back. The literature said nothing of the Macoute Ton-Ton, the private military of Papa Doc, which used murder and intimidation as a means of control. Nor did it mention that, unfortunately, like so many places, skin color was an issue. The lighter skinned, urban mulattos, had most of the money and status. "The Haiti Herald" I bought in 1977 had a front page article entitled, "An American Homesick for Haiti" supposedly written by a grandmother filled with Polly Anna observations on Haiti and its people. Even granted that charity workers are programmed to see the misery and tourists are programmed to see the fun, there was no reconciling what would be my experience in Haiti with hers. The article sounded like it was written by a publicist and gave a stern warning at its conclusion about not using any portion of the article without the grandmom's permission. Why would an honest tourist object to anyone quoting them on the good news? The Caribbean as a whole has little to offer the world but pretty beaches and beautiful sunsets. They are out of the oil for technology cycle. Yet wherever the Caribbean is going, Haiti will get there first. It might be noted that Haiti is the principal world supplier of oil of vetiver. Vetiver is a grass, and its oil is used in aromatherapy. It gives an earthy, woody, smokey smell. Not having experienced it, I can neither endorse nor disclaim it.

I know before I ever began to accumulate things that there would be waste. Things that looked valuable in Houston turned out to be quite useless on site. I purchased an ice-making device (Redi-ice) from Edmund Scientific knowing that a cool drink in the tropics can increase your productivity. This bag fit atop a large cylinder of CO_2 (20 lbs. At $75.00) and made only 4 quarts sized bags of dry ice. All equipment must be evaluated in terms of weight, bulk, utility, and one's ability to operate it and have it repaired.

As in Yucatan, initial preparation for Haiti included hundreds of letters, months of slow buying and price comparison, and thousands of hours of worrying. I believe worrying does help. It fulfills a rehearsal function. Does not even nature attempt to prepare us for death through illnesses, accidents and the death of others?

I explained by letter to the Haitian tourist agencies that I would like to motor throughout Haiti so that none of the beauty of their country would escape me. I received letters from only 2 of the 4 agencies. Neither spoke to the matter of touring restrictions. One sent a map, and the other sent a few tourist brochures. The Haitian information service in Houston, the Haitian Consul in New Orleans, and the Embassy in Washington, D.C. were all unclear on whether there would be any restrictions in travel. It was obvious that no one felt competent to speak for the government. This is usually the case when government employees serve at the pleasure of a dictator rather than through laws and a constitution.

As time drew near to actually go to Haiti, people who had earlier vowed to support me vanished, but the same had occurred just before Yucatan's implementation date.

CHAPTER 11

ARRIVAL IN HAITI

The round trip airfare out of Houston was $296 and went through Miami. We left on August 8, 1975. The first trip was primarily to select a village, to gather information on their problems and resources, and to establish contacts that might be of help. I had decided I'd finance this project, as I did that of Yucatan, by withdrawing my retirement and by monthly savings. As I had quit my job in Milwaukee for Yucatan, I would leave my job in Galveston County for Haiti.

From the airport, Port-au-Prince looks quite pretty. The airport is small but efficient, and when we arrived, we were given a rough, typed list of recommended hotels. In preparation for our reconnaissance, we changed US money into Haitian Gourdes. One telltale sign of a country's affluence is the condition of its paper money. Gourdes were even dirtier and more tattered than India's rupees. It gave you the feeling you needed to wash your hands after handling it. On entering, Customs handled our bags efficiently, taking no interest in the powdered milk and other rapport building gifts, I believe they were checking for guns or expensive items to tax.

A tourist sheet we were given at the airport on arrival indicated there were 77 hotels in Port-au-Prince. We selected the Grand Hotel Oloffson because a friend of the anthropologist had wrongly said it was cheap. Immediately en-route, upon leaving the airport, the terrain was covered with shanties made of junk material. The stores were often abandoned and all Port-au-Prince looked as if it needed painting. Once in Port-au-Prince one could see that there was trash everywhere in the street without any evidence of garbage pick-up. The Grand Hotel turned out to be so expensive that we spent only one night there. It was $45.40 per night counting service charge and 5% tax. Each of the rooms was named after a famous person who had supposedly lodged there. I was in the Ann Bancroft Room. While the room could have used an air conditioner, it was only equipped with a ceiling fan. But at least with the high ceiling fans, the heat had someplace to go. The bed was rather lumpy and felt like a futon, as though it was stuffed with a mixture of rags and clay. The Oloffson however, was an excellent place to make contacts. We had a drink with the nice New York gent managing the hotel, and he advised me to pick another country to do charity work. I can't recall his name, but the receipt for the Grand Hotel Oloffson said A.A. Seitz, owner.

His reasons were rather vague, though essentially clustered around the futility of it all. He introduced us to the Vice-Minister of Tourism, an Aubelin Jolicoeur. This man was later described in a Houston Post as a "man of mystery." He was a journalist, art collector, critic, and survivor of many political purges in Haiti. He took us to his home to meet his French wife and to see the art he had collected and wanted to re-sell at a high profit. His home was in one of the few non-ghetto areas of Port-au-Prince. Attached to his house was a private art gallery with perhaps 200 paintings. He had a reputation for buying cheap from street artists and re-selling at considerable gain. He had been portrayed in the movie version of "The Comedians", starring Richard Burton and Elizabeth Taylor. I know little of art, but his paintings seemed gaudy to me, so I feinted mild interest in them. Jolicoeur said to go to the Northwest Department we needed special permission. He made out the papers for us the following day, but neglected to sign them. He was a survivor. We moved once more to save money before finally finding the Coconut Villa Motel. It was modern, cheap, totally lacking in the character of the Grand Oloffson. While in Port-au-Prince we did almost all travel by the ever-present tap-tap (10 cents a ride – I have wondered in years gone by what the increased price of gasoline has done to the tap-tap and its customers), a small pickup with a canopy over the bed, which had a bench seat on either side. Traveling around Port-au-Prince in a tap-tap was a pleasant experience. When you climbed into the pickup, everyone would politely say "Bon Jour". As they exited, people would frequently, softly say "merci". I had taken a very brief French lesson prior to going to Haiti, but I had a very small vocabulary. A tap-tap gives you the opportunity to meet people from the streets, not that you are ever alone in Haiti. It was impossible to go for even a brief walk without having boys pestering you to become your guide, or women offering prostitution services. In addition, if you wandered into the city's Iron Market, a huge warehouse type building chiefly selling art, the pressure made Mexican markets looks resistive to selling you anything. I bought several paintings there. The paintings were all modern, primitive, or impressionistic. At the Coconut Villa ($28.95 per day), we met a Baptist Missionary from South Carolina, a Reverend Edward J. Corn, who had just returned from the Northwest. Repeatedly he just described it as "unbelievable", whether he was talking about the hunger or the rocky road getting there. To our dismay, we learned that the papers Jolicoeur had given us, even if signed, would not be sufficient to take us to the Northwest. We were told that we needed supplemental papers from another bureau with accompanying photographs. The anthropologist and I hadn't brought any photographs, so spent hours having some poor quality shots made. With these in hand, we once again tried to obtain permission. We walked from agency to agency, trying the Ministry of Tourism,. The Ministry of the Interior, and the Ministry of Foreign Affairs, and always the answer was "No". We were not alone. An American photographer was also trying to obtain permission. He was commissioned to take photos for a German magazine, Stern, I believe, but also received "No" as an answer. The Time article had been an embarrassment, and Haitian officials were not going to look uncaring again. I was told, too, that the government feared revolutionaries in areas that they had little contact with. During the time of Pappa Doc, eight well armed men had formed a revolutionary force and Pappa Doc had begun to pack his bags when the revolutionaries lost their nerve and held up in the armory rather than pressing their advantage, whereupon they were surrounded and executed. Besides, no tourist attempted traveling to the Northwest, thus any traveler there was obliged when he stopped in a town, to report his business and to notify them upon his departure. The entire Northwest Department had not one tourist. They may have never had a tourist. Any tourist heading straight north would have taken a plane from Port-au-Prince to Cap-Haitian. There was an instant way to sort the hoi poloi from the elite. Anyone speaking creole rather than French was automatically pigeon-holed as a person of little significance. The American's "guide" was one the government had hired and had a wealthier, sophisticated look about him. The photographer implied that his guide was more in charge of him than the reverse. Days of fruitless inquiry passed and we began to frequent the private agencies such as Red Cross, along Harry Truman Boulevard. We hoped to gain some advice or get into the forbidden area under the auspices of an established group. We also tried AID (Agency for International Development) and were referred to the American Consultant. They were polite, but said there was nothing they could do to help. The American authorities seemed frustrated by their inability to deal effectively with the Haitian system.

Finally, the anthropologist and I settled for papers that would allow us to travel to the northern city of Cap Haitian. If I could not get into the Northwest, I would select a village as close to the area as possible. I had schemed, too, that if necessary, we would begin the trip to the north, secretly swinging west, hoping for the best. In our first attempt to rent a car, we were told none were available. To admit that you wanted to take one of their precious cars over the roads to the Northwest insured there being no car available to you. Yet fate was kind. We met Dr. William Fougere, Director of the Haitian American Community Help Organization (HACHO) and Xavier St.-Louis, Governor of the Northwest Department. Dr. Fougere, a large, debonair, mulatto physician, was obviously over-burdened, yet upon hearing of our business, gave us the assistance we so badly needed. He looked at the papers, called Laissez-Passer, and said, "I see no problem; you have travel papers for Cap Haitian. It doesn't say what route you will take there." While his logic was not wasted on me, I expressed concern over how other authorities might receive that same argument. To expedite matters, Dr. Fougere loaned us his car, a Cherokee station wagon, and his chauffer, with orders to go where we wished, and stay as long as needed. The Governor of the Northwest Department, Xavier Saint-Louise, who we had the opportunity to meet, seemed equally anxious to help and said, "I am at your service". I was overwhelmed with gratitude. In retrospect, Dr. Fougere was either one of the most powerful people in the country, or someone who was willing to take responsibility, or probably both.

Since I spoke no French or Creole, and the anthropologist spoke very little, we had need of an interpreter because the chauffer spoke no English. Interpreters in Port-au-Prince are as numerous as beggars, and are often the same. However, it is wise to select with some care. We did not want an "official" interpreter and a man that had approached us at the Grand Hotel Oloffson was intimidating and had the look of a Ton-Ton thug about him. The anthropologist and I engaged one of the many streets guides but when we were ready to leave Port-au-Prince, at 7:30 am the following morning, he had not shown. Therefore the driver, the anthropologist, an agricultural advisor J. St. Fort, (who spoke no English who worked for HACHO), and I left, rather than delay the long trip. I didn't want to take any chances on losing our car or driver. The trip to the Northwest would have been near impossible without the chauffer. We were frequently stopped at checkpoints near Port-au-Prince and three times thereafter, and the driver would say, "HACHO", sometimes showing the papers, and we would be passed. I had the feeling that you could have shown them a high school diploma for the papers, particularly one with a gold seal, as they generally could not read. The main problem of roads in Port-au-Prince had been that they were pockmarked, but they were at least paved. Immediately upon leaving the capital, the roads turned to dirt and very soon, the dirt car tracks numbered in the dozens, heading in every direction. In addition, there were no signs whatsoever. If you did not know which was the right track, you would need a compass, or try and follow the coast. The area became increasingly dry as we headed north. There were many cacti from long drought periods. There were vast stretches with no one from whom to ask directions and there were no signposts, just as there were few street signs even in Port-au-Prince. It was not unlike, in that regard, rural America where directions are given more often based on what buildings are there or who lives nearby.

We stopped at a small store in one of the towns, and being hungry, I bought one of the only sandwiches they had. It was cheese with dust on the cover; still it went down and stayed there.

We went through a little town called Pettit Paradise, but if that was a little paradise, then I have greatly misjudged Heaven and Hell. It did have a small cluster of trees and some coconuts. As we went through the large town of Gonaives, it had the look of a town that once had considerable population from the many buildings. However, the streets were sparsely populated, and there was no sign of economic life. While there was a distribution center in Gonaives, the center was crowded and by that time, the street beggars were left behind. There was no one to beg from, and people did not deplete their precious energy doing so. We left enough powdered milk at the distribution center to make 100 quarts and left. We continued through coastal settlements finding a fishing co-op that HACHO had started and a Red Cross representative. The few rural agencies were overwhelmed. We saw distended stomachs, skin that had lost its elasticity, and red hair marking protein deficiencies. Most of the Northwest had been denuded of forest long ago to provide charcoal for cooking fires. It was an ecological disaster and a budding young desert. The few intrepid tourist that journey North from Port-au-Prince did so by plane rather than car. The entire Northwest had a population of 306,869. We were stopped at three separate police stations, were obliged to give our passport numbers and to state our reason for being in the Northwest.

We felt obligated to press on to the furthest point of the area. The trip was hot, long, and dusty. We finally arrived at our end destination, Mole St. Nicholas at 8:30 pm, 13 hours after we had left Port-au-Prince. Mole was the place Christopher Columbus landed in 1492 in his discovery of Hispaniola. There we spent two nights with a Father John Breslin, a Catholic priest from New York who ran a Church, hospital, and pharmaceutical dispensary. John specialized in burns and TB cases. He was a slightly built, tall, pale man who lived very humbly. His house light was the size of a flashlight bulb, and gave very little illumination. A classic philosopher once suggested that the only time you are really doing something for others is when you really do not want to do it. All other times it involved self-interest. If that is the case, John Breslin was certainly there for the people. I did not get the feeling he liked the people or that they liked him. He continually carped about their playing soccer and stirring up dust where he hung his washed clothes. Despite any discord, when someone was sick or injured, he was the first person they came to, and he never failed to render aid as best he could. Shortly before we arrived, a coconut had fallen and hit a woman on the head, rendering her unconscious. Father John treated the concussion. On the premises was a little girl named Marie Jan whom he treated like his own daughter. He paid her 15 centimes for every bedbug she found in each of our beds. She found 24 bedbugs in my bed and she made 90 cents for the effort, a good wage. As far as I can remember, we slept well, without itching. If we had known what was in store, we would have not slept so well. Haiti was known for having a full spectrum of diseases. As we slept, the female Anopheles mosquito bit us both.

At the time, there were only eight doctors in the entire country of Haiti outside of Port-au-Prince. John was not a doctor but had pharmaceutical training, which qualified him highly all things considered. There were no doctors at all, in the Northwest Department. Like in so many of the other third-world countries the missionaries and other sophisticated Westerners have to do the best they can. They do well to take a PDR, a Merck Manual, a good supply of medicines from the capital, and pray for the best. It is also good to pre-identify the major diseases and take meds for them. Anyone wanting to practice need only begin seeing patients at will. If there are any laws in the books of the capital forbidding the practicing of medicine without a license, they are just ignored. It actually works out amazingly well. The poor of those areas cannot afford a doctor, and most doctors appear to have little desire to deal with the poor. No one I know medically unqualified has elected to try major operations (though tooth extractions are considered cricket). My own guidelines, developed over a period, were simplistic but often gave a great deal of relief and are not usually placebos. If the patient had a temperature without alternating chills in a malaria area, I gave a broad-spectrum antibiotic. If he had diarrhea (unless an infant, in which case I try to go with more mild medication), then I administer Lomotil. I always carry worm medicine and painkillers. Chiefly however, people's medical condition benefits from sufficient food. Father Breslin's facility was on the outskirts of town. He charged minimal amounts, and often treated free. He had a windjammer electrical system, running water, and indoor toilets, all of which made his home an oddity. Though Mole St. Nicholas was once a major town in Haiti, it had no electricity. Further, there was not one telephone in town. There was a rough airport but only military aircraft landed there, and that was rare. At this town, the agricultural advisor left us by helicopter to meet with important officials. In retrospect, I would not be surprised if the sole purpose of his being there was to give a report on our activities. It is the type of thing that happens when a government is very paranoid. He was apparently on very important business as the estimate was that Haiti's Air Force was composed of five to six helicopters and only about a half a dozen propeller driven planes. The houses built in Mole were seemingly left by the French, and while a few approached being grand, they took on a pretty but ghostly aura with only the illumination of the moon. As everywhere in Haiti, the food imported and packaged, is outrageous in price. As a rule, the price seems to be double the price we pay in the United States. An $0.85 can of Spam would cost $1.70 there. Bottled beer that would have cost you $0.50 in the United States went for $1.00. Only homegrown items like beans and rice were cheap. As far as I could tell, in the entire Northwest, there was not one movie theater, not one nightclub, not one TV or social club, not one hotel, not even one restaurant as we know them. There were no sounds of music or radio, nothing but small group conversation and an occasional dog barking. Ninety percent of the population spoke Creole, which presented a problem with French being favored by the government and upper class. While in the Northwest, the people seemed too lethargic from deprivation to be called friendly, but all were polite if resigned to whatever came.

In route back we went through the small settlement of Baie de Henne. It had a population of about 700. Like the rest of the Northwest, it was an ecological disaster. Much of the broader area had been denuded of trees to make charcoal, which was sold in Port-au-Prince. On the road from Mole St. Nicholas in the far north, is a town named Bombardopolis only 12 miles away with a nurse, though I learned nothing of her qualifications. The small town of Baie de Henne seemed to best meet my qualifications, although any village in Haiti may have done as well. Having made a selection, we returned to Port-au-Prince.

While the anthropologist and I waited to fly to the states, we spent time touring the poorer sections of Port-au-Prince. The poorest place we found was next to the sea and was called Cite Simone Wharf Cabotage.

People that lived at the Cite Simone, if they were lucky, had four poles and a piece of cloth to go across the top to form a shelter from the sun. They were crammed in like sardines, and at night, the groans would begin. There is no welfare system in Haiti. Everyone is left to his or her own devices or nature. Just outside their living area was an open area where they, if they could find the strength, would go to defecate. Have you ever wondered what people would do without underwear, toilet paper, soap, food, or medicine when they get sick? I would like to ask the people themselves, but we live and talk on such different planes that my naïve questions would only shame me, and I doubt I would receive answers I would understand. Just outside this center of poverty is somewhat better off. They may eat garbage and do without what most of us consider necessities, but there is life among them. They live in houses with tin walls and dirt floors, but have relationships with other human beings. Their relationships may be manipulative, subservient, or dishonest, but they are people who are not completely invisible. They may go to church or be hired for spot jobs occasionally. They are often healthy enough to be completely ambulatory, and they are aware of the existence of others. They hear voices instead of the slow contractions of their own stomachs, and on Sunday night, they throw together makeshift nightclubs (a wind-up record player and a 60-watt bulb surrounded by four pieces of tin). Patrons were charged a nickel for admission. They even sometimes patronize the tiny stores that sell items like used glass jars, the kind we throw away when the peanut butter is all gone. Just outside the city, along the coast, is a string of houses of prostitution with exotic names like the Copacabana.

Also while in Port-au-Prince I made inquiries along the wharfs as to whether I could hire a man to drop me along with my materials in Baie de Henne. I first approached a Captain Pierre who ran a motor launch to Isle de La Gonave when there were a sufficient number of passengers. While he had never gone to the Northwest, he expressed a willingness to do so for $350.00. I then went to the boats behind the casino. They wanted $300.00. Lastly, I returned to Cite Simone where I found leaky, old wooden boats going to the Northwest for as cheap as $10.00. They were sailboats with no restroom or cooking facilities, and I was told it would take 3-4 days to get there.

On Saturday night, a special night for voodoo, we went to a ceremony on the outskirts of Port-au-Prince. There were perhaps 30 worshippers in the ceremony, which was preceded by a man making white chalk powder designs and sketchings on the ground. The worshippers were dressed all in red except for two priests, who dressed in white. There was a small bonfire in the center at the ceremony, which began slow enough, but gained in intensity, and lasted perhaps 2 hours. Eighteen looked as though they were possessed during the ceremony. One woman, who appeared to have a fit of sorts, climbed into a tree above where we were sitting and we moved, thinking she might fall upon us. The priest would take a mouthful of cheap rum and spray it into the face of a worshipper. One of the men did something that seemed astounding. He ate part of a glass, and while I was a bit surprised, I'd heard of this before. Then, he took a chicken, pulled its head off, chewed on the body, and got a mouthful of feathers. He then drank blood from the main portion of the chicken's neck and swallowed the feathers, quill and all. But what really surprised me was what he did next. He reached into the fire, grabbing a 4" diameter log that had been burning for some time. He held the log by the cool end, but where the coals were hottest, in the center, he appeared to take several large bites with no damage we could see to his mouth. Shortly afterwards the ceremony ended.

One of the more interesting contacts we made was a Reverend Luc Nere. Dad had corresponded with him so that my parents might sponsor a Haitian child through his organization called Aid Aux Enfants. He claimed 900 children would gather at their pavilion each Saturday for a decent meal one time a week. He claimed he could feed, clothe and educate a child for $10.00 per month. He was a Baptist minister but no ordinary Bible thumper. He ran a radio station in Soto which was a town considered the voodoo capital. He also had a clinic for infants in Port-au-Prince, and his son was the chief physician of the clinic.

I asked Luc how the people at Cite Simone survived and he said, "By a miracle." The subject then turned to the voodoo ceremony we'd seen. The anthropologist asked Luc, "Can voodoo priests take away demons?" He replied, "Yes, but only the demons they put there in the first place." I said, "Luc, the possessions appeared epileptic in nature." Without hesitation he said, "That's right, and as long as you call it epilepsy, you'll never cure it." He seemed to imply that it was not a question of something leaving the brain that belonged there through pre-microscopic lesions. Rather it was perhaps a case of something entering the brain that did not belong there.

Luc said the customs duty could be waived when bringing equipment into the country by obtaining a franchise. However, a complete listing of materials must be sent, and the material must wait at the custom's station for one month prior to release. If duty was paid the material could usually be cleared immediately. While the amount of duty could be bargained upon, it could go as high as twice the value of the goods. I wondered about his earlier statement that the duty "could" be waived, and that the material could "usually" be cleared. Words like "try", "usually" and "could" always catch my attention. Then too, the procedure was too reminiscent of the debacle at the beginning of the Yucatan project when I was assured that a complete listing arriving 6 weeks in advance would clear my path.

We gave our flashlights and a few other items we had retained to two women sitting on a doorstep that were delighted to get them. Shortly thereafter I flew out, with the anthropologist electing to stay a little longer.

After I returned home I began to develop a fever. And when I'd come from the shower to bed, I'd get racking chills that a stack of blankets could not immediately stop. When my temperature rose to 105 degrees I drove to my parents' house concerned since at 106 degrees, you begin to get into brain damage. It was unfortunate that I displayed no symptoms in Haiti. They would have known right away what the problem was seeing it so often. I was driven to Hermann Hospital in Houston where I was put through a long series of repetitive questions while suffering a tremendous headache. It was good there was no gun handy. I am not sure I would not have shot myself. I was placed in a room while the lab technicians did their marvelous work.

The anthropologist, having returned and heard I was ill, called the hospital and told me she had suffered a bout of malaria. She recognized the symptoms from having contracted it in Samoa, and recovered quickly from the right meds. I had been begging the staff for antibiotics, which would have done no good. When I reported what the anthropologist had told me, the doctor seemed irritated and emphatically announced, "You do not have malaria." They had a conference on my case being a teaching hospital, and only one doctor said, "We can't totally rule out malaria." He said so, I believe, in response to my spleen being very hard. The doctor, who had announced so assuredly that I did not have malaria, came in and informed me that I had a classic case of typhoid fever. My room instantly became an isolation room. A strange phenomenon occurred. My sense of smell became extraordinarily keen. While I normally don't have much of a sense of smell, a nurse could stand at the door and I would get nauseated from her perfume. One came in to fluff my pillow and I said,

"Your perfume." She said, "Isn't it wonderful, everyone likes it." My reply would have required that I take a breath, but it would seem that my head turned to the side and a pained expression on my face would have told her something.

Four days after being hospitalized, I was told they were sure of the diagnosis: vivax malaria. The lab had finally completed the difficult task of finding it.

The pompous doctor came to my room, sat next to my bed and without a word of apology read a long article on malaria and the particular mosquito that carries it. I was to learn later it was the number one disease on earth. Twenty-five million adult Africans suffered from malaria, not counting the children and those who peopled South America and the tropical east. Given the number of people infected, I wondered why he so cavalierly dismissed the chances of my being among them. The isolation gear was immediately removed and I soon began to feel a little better. Recovery was not immediate however. Still it was not without benefit. In the process I eventually lost 30 pounds and could fly around the track field, as I'd not been able to since early teens. Before beginning the Haitian project I told a friend I'd rather die than not see it through. So malaria was a price I was willing to pay.

CHAPTER 12

Preparing for the project to actually be undertaken in Haiti, I made the decision to return without the anthropologist. She was a good person and highly intelligent, but I had no clue she had the slightest concern about God. And when I would undertake such a work, I decided I need all the help I could get. To go on such a project with what I believed to be an agnostic, was simply bad juju. Still, I did not fancy going alone. To go alone would mean there would be no one to go for help if I had a medical emergency, so for my next travel companion, I chose the 19 year-old son of a friend. I believe his father thought such a trip might instill higher values in the boy and help him find direction. At age 17 I was sent by my father to East Africa to stay with distant relatives. The trip had made a world of difference in me. I found young Al Ruscelli to be a bright boy, filled with courage and eagerly anticipating adventure.

In preparation for the journey I again contacted the Haitian Embassy in Washington, and the Haitian Information Office in Houston, which still could not tell me who was in charge of the customs department there, or whether special permission would continue to be needed to go to the Northwest. The Information officer had not been back to his country in over a year, and confessed their information would be obsolete. Apparently, under the Duvalier Regime, officials served totally at the pleasure of Jean-Claude Duvalier. To have funds for the work, I followed through with my plan to quit my job and drew out the money for retirement, which had accumulated in a mutual fund. The years of working in Yucatan had taught me a lot, just not enough. Early on, it was becoming plain that Haiti would be more isolated, more backwater than Yucatan.

I knew I wanted lots of seed, and bought tropical, exotic seeds from all over the world through mail order sources. I had seed from China, India, Africa, and Australia. I purchased two 300 foot seeming nets, gallon containers of diarrhea medicine, a tiny motor for a small boat, large amounts of food that required no refrigeration, and a large trunk of medicines (10,000 aspirin, antibiotics, parasite meds, etc.) with clothing, blankets, 7 cast nets, rods and reels and whatever else I thought might have utility. There was very little I could count on being able to buy in Haiti, even if I took the time to shop. Linda sewed 16 oversized duffle bags from blue jean material, and in accordance with dad's suggestion, I labeled each bag and had an invoice of what it contained. His experience of working on the docks as a young man paid off.

Each bag was stretched and crammed full. In all, they weighted over 1,200 pounds. Aware it would not be feasible to convey it by air, I decided to try and go by sea. I began asking about sailboats for charter out of Galveston, but soon gave up on that idea. As fate would have it, I found a freighter that made Port-au-Prince a regular port call. It even left from nearby New Orleans. The ship was named The Suriname after the tiny South American Country of its registry. The one-way cost was $155.00, which seemed very reasonable to me. I'd planned that we would return by air once the work was done.

My faithful dad announced that he planned to take vacation time and come with us. I was to learn however, that the schedule of freighters is quite elastic. At any time, they might receive a message to diverge from their planned route to pick up a load elsewhere before returning to their scheduled stops. Only the Line Manager could give an estimate of when they might arrive.

As the day approached for the ship to arrive in New Orleans, delay followed delay. Dad had his vacation set in stone so while I still awaited the Suriname, his vacation date was upon us.

He then decided he should go to Haiti alone, and be my point man. He would make such contacts as he could and gather other current information. We generally found that people on missions of charity are well received. Though we felt frustrated by our separation, it actually worked out very well.

Al and I left for New Orleans just before the Suriname was to arrive. The pick up with a camper was loaded with Linda, her father, Al and I, plus all the bags. It was a tight squeeze and Al rode in the back most of the way. Linda and her father would drive the pick up back upon emptying it.

Even though the New Orleans freight-company told me I could store anything that would fit in our cabin, they recanted when they learned how much luggage we had. It's true that the cabin was small and I knew it would be tight from ceiling to floor, but I'd hoped to keep everything in sight. Additionally, I was informed I'd have to pay freight charges on all but personal luggage. Too, I'd have to have a Bill of Laden, and go through a freight forwarder to obtain it. Luckily, there was one in the same building, who indicated he might be willing to expedite matters in view of the circumstances.

Even at that, he insisted we first give a list of the goods to the Haitian Consulate and pick up authorized import forms. He said the equipment should be properly crated but that it might be arranged to store our things on top of everything else that was going into the hole of the ship.

We found the Haitian Consulate in the low rent area right around the corner. The Consul seemed idle as Consuls go. He charged me an import fee of 2%, but allowed me to set the value of my materials. He also charged me $3.00 for the nine forms we were required to use. The Consul closed our meeting by telling us there would be no further duties, which led me to question his experience, competence, or honesty. Getting through Customs with that quantity of equipment is never easy anywhere.

When we returned to the freight forwarders, he typed the list onto the Bill of Laden and forms given to us by the Consulate. This was the only service performed but charged a goodly amount for the trifle. By this time I was feeling frustrated by what seemed like an amateurish way the various authorities handled our needs. To add to our angst, the line informed me that though the ship was at dock, we would not be able to board until it was ready to leave. It was moving up and down the dock loading. They suggested we stay at the nearby motel until sailing. The forwarder also suggested we carry our equipment to the dock warehouse and leave it there until we were able to depart. He told us to be sure to get a receipt from the warehouse.

When we located the warehouse the man in charge told us he would not give us a receipt and did not want to be responsible for the materials. Looking at the vast quantity of boxes in the warehouse, I wondered how anything ever got delivered to the correct destination by ship.

The warehouseman did suggest that we talk to the Suriname's First Mate to see if we could load the bags ourselves. I've rarely found anyone where they are supposed to be. Moving around on a job seems to be an unofficial way of taking a quasi break and preserve one's sanity. After making inquiry, I'd have settled for the ship's cook. But, luckily, we found the Second Mate who gave us permission to load the materials aboard in a storage locker above deck. I mumbled thanks to God, and was ecstatic with controlled joy as we, and the crew, put the materials in locked storage.

Upon returning to the freight forwarder, we told him we'd loaded everything ourselves. He said, "You can't do that." We assured him it was a feit accompli and he just shrugged.

Al and I bid farewell to Linda and her father and walked to the motel. She cried and I felt like it. Would I ever see her again I wondered.

I found by phone, the following day, that dad had met with Dr. Fougere who suggested we bring our materials in through HACHO. Since the materials were for charitable purposes, that would mean free entry.

The next day we were allowed to sleep on the ship but we were told the freighter would not leave until its air conditioner was fixed. The air conditioner was old and they were having difficulty finding parts. The Suriname itself was 17 years of age. It looked much older.

We were nevertheless, glad to board. We were sick of fast foods and watching TV in the cheap motel room. Al had gone out on the town a bit the night before and had seen a dead woman on the street in the French Quarter. From previous years I was already tired of the gaudiness of New Orleans. Besides, I think we were both a little too focused on Haiti to feel like recreating ourselves.

The ship's crew looked swarthy and like movie cut throats. Yet I found that beneath that exterior, they were child-like in many respects. They represented a range of mixed ethnicities and almost to a man slammed the idea of ever marrying. They distrusted women, and only wanted a small, shady, comfortable place, for themselves on land. Some dreamed of having a chicken farm attached to a highway restaurant, far from the sea. One estimated that his little piece of such heaven would cost $15,000. They all wanted to avoid responsibilities. But until they could realize their dream they were glad to have a good paying job.

In accordance with company policy, the First Mate had his wife aboard for the trip – a yearly perk. The poor woman, with one child, stayed sea sick most of the journey and rarely left her cabin. That was probably a wise policy since she was the only woman aboard a ship with all men.

The Captain, Emile, looked in dress like a common laborer. He was 34, part Negro and part Caucasian. He had a Yul Brenner manner of confidence, and had been given a thoroughbred education on the sea in Holland. Suriname had been a Dutch Colony before finally gaining its independence. Emile thought his education was too theoretical, but he was the envy of others who aspired to command on the ocean. He was one of only 4 Captains in the small nation of 300,000.

While waiting for the air conditioner part, we had a wonderful opportunity to observe the loading. They loaded five new cars on the ship and Emile said there would be a 62% duty, plus freight charges. Occasionally a new bag of rice burst open and pigeons would zoom in to eat the spillage. We were delayed another day by rain. If the hole had been open when it rained, much of the rice would have been ruined. So much was loaded into the hole that it was obvious that my equipment would have been smashed had it been under the tonnage we took on.

At last a part was found for the air conditioner. We legally met the requirements for departure even though the air output was less than a person's breath.

The ship's cook said, "You like rice? We got plenty of rice." A truer statement was never uttered. Each meal might have a modest portion of meat, but there was always a great, bulbous heap of rice garnished by the flies that made the Suriname their home.

CHAPTER 13

A SEA VOYAGE TO PORT-AU-PRINCE

After what felt like years, the Suriname set sail from New Orleans. I'd always thought of the city as being right on the Gulf of Mexico, but it took 8 slow hours to clear the Mississippi Delta.

As we approached the sea, leaving behind the city and coastal lights, how dark the night grew. But just as I began to wonder what I was doing there, the stars broke through the clouds and I felt close to God.

Once at sea, Emile had more time to visit with us and to tell us tales of the sea, his country, and his family. He was well known in Suriname and had a common complaint about small communities. Everyone knew his personal business. He liked to flaunt society and rebel in small, mischievous ways like resisting social functions, dressing very casual, and refusing to marry. He had once been officially engaged to an Indian girl but refused to become a Hindu. Largely he had a rather adolescent view of women. Those who wanted him, he did not want. His family had long coaxed him to wed, but he preferred carousing with East Indian women and over-indulging with beer. Nothing mattered so much to Emile as his independence. He seemed a little lonely but he recognized this as the flip side of freedom. He dearly loved Suriname and felt he knew every aspect of the country and its people.

He also had the different ethnic groups pigeon holed. He explained that the men from India lived in a very stingy fashion. They either sent their money back to India, or spent it on their home. They ate, in a meager fashion, meals with cheap ingredients, and never took their wives out. The winning line with Indian girls was to offer them an alternative to the way their mothers lived, if only for a day. He described the "Bush Negro" in exactly opposite terms. He said they live for the hour. When they get their hands on money they buy the best of clothes. They eat, drink, and party royally.

As we sat in his cabin drinking the cold beer he generously offered, he waxed on the Bermuda Triangle. He explained that there are far more people in Florida, and the Florida Keyes with money to buy boats, than there are people experienced with the sea. Emile stated that the really peculiar thing about some not returning was that as many came back as did. I asked why more people didn't build a raft or boat to escape such grinding poverty. For at that time, the sea was as level as glass. He told me that in 2 hours time, the sea conditions could radically change. He told stories of would-be escapees dying of thirst and happy to be picked up by anyone, even though they were returned.

About 4 hours after he described the ocean as being capricious, as if to validate his statements, the sea grew very rough. Emile calmly informed us that the weather was often rough between Haiti and Cuba. There was lightning from one horizon to the next, and the waves were so high that the ship that previously felt grand and safe, now seemed little more than a rowboat. At gatherings of Captains, Emile said, you'd sometimes hear them brag of having survived this hurricane, or that storm. Such boasting only displayed poor seamanship. Emile explained that a good Captain does not allow himself to be caught in a hurricane.

Emile expressed no interest in being charitable and yet he seemed very proud of his father trying to get a church built in Suriname, and of his taking a calf into the jungle to try and improve the native stock.

Emile said it was good that I'd earlier given up on the idea of trying to charter a sailboat to Haiti. He mentioned that the currents and the wind would often have run against us, and some days we would make no progress, or even lose ground. He estimated the journey would have taken 3 weeks if I'd made it at all.

He asked if I'd read the book, "The Comedians," and when I told him I had, and asked if he had done so, he said, "Yes, and it even made me afraid to go to Haiti." But, he continued to go and praise the Haitians for their politeness. As a captain, when he entered the room, they all stood. As likeable as he was, I found only one thing annoying about Emile. Over and over again he played the song, "You picked a fine time to leave me Lucille" by Kenny Rogers. I carelessly thought of some voodoo spell to hex the recording but ended just by enduring. The song seemed to be therapeutic for our Captain, reminding him of the dangers of marriage and the wisdom of his choice to stay single. Emile said he did not know if he believed in voodoo or not.

I was grateful not to be seasick. I had experienced that malady only once in my life and I'd rather have a day of Malaria than a day of seasickness.

I'd had little idea of how boring life can be at sea. The deck was too small and chopped up to go for a walk, and while the men worked, (work on deck began at 7:35 A.M.) there was nothing to do but eat, fan the flies, and sleep. Even sleep eluded me. The cabin was so hot that both Al and I developed fever blisters. Attempts to sleep on deck were fouled by what felt like gale force winds.

The motor droned endlessly, monotonously, as we passed Cuba. You never realize how large Cuba is until you begin going around it at about 9 mph, yet, we were right on schedule. Our Captain explained that while small ships can afford to fall slightly behind schedule, the Captain of a large ship is fired if he's unreasonably late.

CHAPTER 14

ARRIVAL

After nearly 5 days at sea, we saw Haiti off the side of our ship, and at 4:20 AM we passed Mole St. Nicholas. How I wish Emile could have let us off there, but to do so would have cost him his career.

By 3:30 PM we slowly pulled into Port-au-Prince with the pilot's assistance. I couldn't believe it. The tall man in a Haitian straw hat standing on the dock was Dad. I could hardly be happier to see Christ himself. Somehow that decorated soldier from Patton's Army always knew when I'd arrive. When asked how, he simply replied, "You were due earlier." The first news he gave me was that he had rented a car and had driven into the Northwest as far as Gonaives with no papers! I never learned exactly how he managed that. In the year of my absence, he explained, a new road had been completed. Too, believing I would accept Dr. Forgerie's offer to bring my goods in through HACHO, he had made a deal with Mr. Placide subject to my approval. I was to learn that Dad had made dozens of important contacts, some vital. When it was finally time to transfer our goods, the dockworkers refused to do so because the bags had no marking other than that which I'd used to number them. It was probably an excuse to get a bribe since once I gave them a small fee the unloading to the warehouse preceded without further difficulty – once they had put their own mark on each bag.

We were told, at dock, that we could take one container ashore. The remainder had to stay aboard awaiting its transfer to the Custom's warehouse.

Al and I went to the ship's storage locker and stuffed packets of seed in the chest holding the medicines. I reasoned the seeds and medicines to be the most important, most irreplaceable items. We then left the ship with the chest and our personal bags. The two Custom's officials grumbled something about it being excessive, but briefly checked the chest, accepted a $10.00 bribe, and let us pass. Dad gave us the card of the hotel we would stay at, and took the chest and bags by taxi thereto.

Emile wanted to take us on a brief tour of the waterfront. Our first stop was the Sunshine Grill, within easy walking distance. I don't believe I've ever seen anything like the Sunshine, before or after that day. If they ever served food at the Sunshine, it must have been long before. It was a bar, crammed with humanity flowing onto the street. Any new comer was immediately set upon by men and women offering anything they felt was marketable. Generally, the men tried to convince you that they had contacts of influence who could obtain whatever you needed. The women, mainly past their prime, were making fellatio gestures and were trying to get patrons into the alley to perform the sexual act of the customer's choosing. All the action at the Sunshine was going at breakneck speed. While there was no traditional entertainment, they would send runners for anything you required. When we left, I believed I'd seen the ultimate in high-pressure sales.

We strolled along a seaside boulevard stopping at a middle class café where the manager tried to keep beggars from bothering the customers, with only partial success.

Emile then hailed a tap-tap, which took us to the outskirts of town to a club named Casablanca. It had the look of Mexican bordello from the outside. Inside were pretty girls in evening gowns. I was told the most popular of these were the light skinned girls from the Dominican Republic. As we left, I noted an expensive looking hotel nearby and wondered what kind of person would stay there. I suspected it was someone wanting to lose themselves in debauchery. I also suspected human life was cheap along that avenue. As we wound down our tour, we bid Emile sincere good wishes for his future. Parting from such good company is always difficult. It is especially true when the person is someone of importance who can get things done and offers a degree of protection. Yet protection is something I have never actually needed. Overwhelmingly, fears are products of the imagination as when a child fears the dark. Yet no one can guarantee that every fear is ill founded. Mainly however, I just missed Emile's good stories and pleasant demeanor. I was to learn that there were some 40 U.S. volunteer agencies active in Haiti in addition to our government's A.I.D. CARE, Church World Services, and Catholic Relief Services operated the largest programs. Countries with bilateral programs included France, Canada, West Germany, Taiwan, and Israel. One would think with so many entities at work there they would be tripping over one another. Yet, they must be a drop in the bucket of need, for during my entire time in Haiti, except for Turbull's Baptist enclave, I never saw a project or benefit. I am unclear on how to explain that.

CHAPTER 15

We then taxied to our hotel in Petionville. The road to Petionville was the only really proper road I found in Haiti. Petionville is a posh area in the hills overlooking the squalor of Port-au-Prince. It is cooler, cleaner, and all the hotels were nice. One was so fancy it even had a small swimming pool for each room. Dad had selected one that was reasonably priced and was on the American plan (meals included). Our new abode was the Sendral Guest House on Rue Sendral, and the proprietor was Rachel Sendral, herself. The old French woman had lived through 3 revolutions in Haiti. That night, we had a meal without rice, flies, or a moving table, and the table was set in elegant, old world fashion.

The Sendral Guest House ($18.00 a day with 2 meals) was a pleasant enclave used by AID and CARE workers as well as low level diplomats. I'm not clear on why there were so few beggars found in Petionville, since the hotels and their guests obviously had some money. Or, why the desperate people below didn't storm the height and remove the heads of the privileged few. I never saw what I recognized as a policeman in Petionville.

At days end, the government and charity workers in Sendral's, as in English colonies of old, would gather for a sundowner beer and discuss problems, or ways of getting things done. Other than a housewife and a few children, no one watched TV. There was an English Language cinema in town, but it too had poor participation. No one ever mentioned a nightclub, the theater, a festival, or any trivial pastimes. We would all retire and rise early as the daylight hours, particularly before the tropical heat, were considered precious.

In discussion with a CARE worker, I was surprised how few paid CARE workers there were worldwide, and they all seemed to know one another. They had their own kind of toughness as their lives consisted of going from one grueling assignment to another.

You could put all the CARE assignments into a bag and you were bound to draw out a bad one. There were no London or Paris stations for them.

The U.S. Government workers seemed less dedicated, more defeated by the bureaucracy of the host country. But in fairness, they were not playing on a level field with the small, private organizations; they were more center-ring. Our government workers were indirectly tied to big money, matters of national power, pride, and politics. To add to their difficulty at being effective, they were on a 2-year duty cycle. By the time they had a grasp of the particular problems of an area, and had begun to form hypothesis of what would work best, it was time for them to leave.

Sendral's was the kind of place where I could have spent years. Everything about it suited me. There were, nevertheless, technical problems from time to time. Mrs. Sendral's handyman and chauffer had been missing for 2 weeks. This meant that when the water quit running, she had to quickly find another man to do the repair. When the water was briefly off, we used water from the swimming pool to flush the toilet. I was told that her chauffer had demonstrated the poor judgment to get into a loud argument with a taxi driver in front of the home of the Chief of Police. It was presumed he was taken to jail. One Haitian told me that sometime when you went to jail, your hands were tied above your head and your lower clothing removed. Then, a man with a paddle came and, "made the fat come through the meat." Sometimes you didn't leave jail alive. It was assumed a similar fate befell the chauffer, since it was most unlikely that he would simply have left on his own. If you were fortunate enough to find a job in Haiti, you didn't vacate it while you lived. Mrs. Sendral was concerned but her inquiries yielded nothing. I liked that elderly lady and she liked me. Rather than respectfully calling her Madam Sendral as the others did, I boldly called her Rachael as though we were contemporaries. She showed me her appreciation by often giving me better cuts of meat or more of it.

By night, when not talking with the organizational diplomats or other functionaries, I would scan the "Haiti Herald". It had some interesting views; I'd like to quote a few from their April 1977 issue. "There is no conflict between Voodoo and Christianity, rather, the two are complementary. The Christian God occupies the pinnacle of the hierarchy of Voodoo deities. Thus the Voodoo goddess, Erzuli, is identified with the Virgin Mary. We suggest you visit the Voodoo temple Le Peristyle De Mariani . . . located six miles south of Port-au-Prince on the Carrefour Road, just before le lambi night club." The publication mentioned "creative driving", "a departure from the mundane world of speed limits and traffic tickets." It also said "Haiti has one of the lowest crime rates in the world. Tourists can feel safe anywhere, any time day or night". And "Haiti's population is about 5 million with 90 percent of the people living in rural areas." The casinos were heavily advertised but I did not think the odds would be good.

Dad's contact with HACHO had informed him that for HACHO to help me, I would have to sign all materials over to that agency. In that way, the Customs officials would understand that they belong to their well-known agency. I have enough paranoia in me to really be nervous about such an arrangement. Once I signed them over, I had no guarantee they wouldn't end up being sent God knows where. They might even end up as some official's black market inventory. But, as Dad wisely advised me, "You've got to trust someone." So, I took a deep breath, and signed them over. Even at that, nothing happened immediately. An AID representative predicted it would partially be stolen. However, he was impotent to help, and said that even the American government had trouble getting equipment into the country. He suggested we hire a guard. That was impossible since a nonofficial would not be allowed to stay in the vast warehouses 24 hours a day. To add to my anxiety, the young AID representative, and others, had stories of material that would never leave the warehouse. Two Frenchmen had paid $10,000 for a car sent to Haiti and the Customs demanded a $20,000 tax. The Frenchmen could not pay the tax and were not allowed to send the car back to its country of origin, so there it sat for years, aging in the warehouse.

I had made various inquiries about how the warehouse could have been avoided. However, the schemes were all silly and too high risk. When I was finally informed my goods were in the warehouse, I went there to see if anything was missing. Customs had miscounted the bags and there had been some confusion from that, but I satisfied myself the bags were all there and stored properly. The warehouses were so vast, and the boxes and crates so many, that it was something of a tribute to their efficiency that they could locate my goods, for I heard yet more stories of clerical errors and actions taking months. By this time I'd been in Haiti for one week. The AID man said if I'd gotten my materials from Customs in a week, it would have been a record.

While waiting, I hired two interpreters. One named Jeannot Remy, was the son of a preacher from the desperately poor wharf area. The other, Wesner Hypolite (who agreed to work for $10.00 per week plus room and board), had been recommended by another local church. Jeannot took us to a nearby orphanage in bad need of funds. The orphanage manager had an old wreck of a car with the driver's door held on by a piece of rope. Their sleeping facilities were dirt floors. When a bag of rice I'd brought dropped and a few grains fell into the dirt, the children carefully picked up each grain. I gave a dollar to each of the children, and right in front of me a larger child angrily took the dollar of a smaller child. My first inclination was to collar the larger child and return it to the smaller one. But the manager did nothing so I also did nothing. Perhaps the dollars all went into a common fund and the large child thought the younger one intended to keep it for him self. In any event I would not be there for long, and any move I made could result in retaliation against the small child.

The orphanage manager also offered to help me get my materials from customs free. It was obvious however, that he was unable to help himself and had no influence in any quarter.

Later that same day, we spent time buying shovel and hoe blades, bulk foods, and large containers of fresh water for Al and me. Just as in the preceding year, everything was expensive. After our buying spree, we hauled everything to our hotel room. If I would have had more time, I probably could have eventually gotten assistance from AID and private agencies such as Services Chretier d' Haiti in terms of small grants or of equipment, but I had a full plate plus I wanted to see what could be done with my money, not someone else's. And, in reading through old notes I had forgotten in how many small ways many people helped. There are so very many people willing to help if it doesn't cost them a lot of time, money, or trouble.

The following morning we toured a facility that had been written up in National Geographic. It was a missionary station run by a Baptist named Wallace Turnbull. It was like a small piece of America set down in the outskirts of Port-au-Prince. Included was a school, students' dormitories, a souvenir shop, and a large plant nursery. This was the kind of operation that could be put together only with many contacts and years of work. Wallace and his family were bright and knew Haiti as few others did. He gave me the exact location of where he thought I could find water in Pettit Paradise and Baie de Henne along with the names of contacts in the Northwest.

As always seems to occur with people who have the grit to get things done under adverse conditions, I found him opinionated and strong as garlic. He had the belief that many Haitians were slow witted because of malnutrition. He maintained they rarely take personal responsibility in failure. If something breaks, the explanation is "It broke," never "I broke it." If excessive rainfall washes something away, it is because of spirits, never because erosion measures were not taken. Wallace said if they can't understand it, it is either a trick to them (which is alright because dishonesty is rewarded), or magic – no science.

CHAPTER 16

To my surprise, and everyone else's, the following day, 9 days after our arrival in Port-au-Prince, our goods were released from Customs. Mr. Placide came to the warehouse just to facilitate our finishing with Customs. His assistance greatly expedited matters. We went from one duty station to another, finally receiving 21 minister stamps and permission to take our equipment and go. There were no significant fees connected to the transaction. It was obvious that my marriage to HACHO was blessed. It was equally obvious it was an organization with power in a country where it was hard to tell who had power over what.

I had a sigh of relief after we cleared Customs and hired porters to cart the bags to taxis to the HACHO facility and to take us to the guesthouse.

Soon after, I was told that a Pastor Edgar Shreeve would take, Al, me, and half the equipment to Baie de Henne. Dr. Fougere had agreed to send the other half, with the two interpreters, immediately thereafter.

Dad was at the end of his vacation and so he flew back to Houston. His work was done, and done well, but mine was just beginning.

In the morning we stuffed goods into every corner of Edgar's truck with him mildly carping at the weight and size of the load. To our surprise, he already had 2 passengers. We had a flat before we cleared Port-au-Prince. But that was par for a missionary working in one of the poorest countries on earth. We managed to make it to a service station where they changed it.

I insisted on paying all our expenses en route. Gasoline was 97 cents a gallon, which was expensive for that time. Our meals included eating stale cheese sandwiches at bars, and chasing them with hot sodas.

On leaving Port-au-Prince, it was obvious massive intensive work had been done on the road north just as Dad had said. I was very gratified.

During the trip Edgar railed against communism, and except for its antireligious posture, I'm not sure what that was about. I doubt Edgar knew all the sources of his vitriol himself. I don't think he knew much about communism, and was certainly unwilling to give it credit for anything.

When we finally arrived at Gonaives, we had a chance to eat at the Rex Restaurant, a genuine, sit down eatery. It was clean, we were the only customers, and the service was the slowest I've found on earth.

We made a brief stop at Pettit Paradise, about 13 kilometers from Baie de Henne, locating the place where Wallace Turnbull said we'd find water. Edgar showed us his name written in cement where he had once helped the people establish a sealed water well, but the pump no longer worked. Additionally, he said that the water tasted bad - like decaying vegetation. I left a hand pump there for them to use if they found better water or decided to use the water they found regardless of taste.

Next in our journey, we came to a settlement called Pettit Anse. From our road high on the hill we could see it far below. The village was a tiny peninsula jutting out into the sea. I could see little hope for this village. It was located in one of those areas that would have been pleasant enough for a picnic, but was never meant to be inhabited. It consisted of a cluster of stick houses setting at the far end of the barren, hot, dune-surrounded homes. Just where the peninsula began, however, there were a few green trees, certainly salt water tolerant.

CHAPTER 17

ARRIVAL IN THE VILLAGE

When we arrived at Baie de Henne twelve hours after leaving Port-au-Prince, how different it was from the way I remembered it. On the first trip we had only motored through a coconut grove on the outskirts and missed the town's center. It was much larger than I'd known, with many more buildings. Most of the buildings had dirt floors and were old, badly in need of paint. Since there was no electricity, they did little more than shield the citizenry from the sun and rain. The buildings looked of French construction and though they'd once been elegant, I thought perhaps the floors had rotted out. As in Yucatan, I'd come to Haiti with thousands of one-dollar bills and had gotten as many 10 Gourde notes as possible. The exchange note was 5 gourdes to the dollar.

Shortly after our arrival, the other half of our goods came, with the two interpreters. I was to find only one man in the area that spoke a little English. This 72 year old was the father of the commandant of the local Ton-Tons. He had worked in Cuba in the past. Within the first couple of days of being in Baie de Henne, I had to report our presence to the authorities as though our arrival had not been the big event of the year. The "authority" turned out to be the father of the commandant of the Ton-tons. He was a dignified, tall, thin man, unassuming and polite. Arrangements were made for us to stay at the home of the local Baptist preacher who was away at the time. The house was sturdy with a tin roof and separate sections. The preacher's wife was there and gave Al and me each a bedroom with a cement floor while she and her family took the large bedroom on the other side of the kitchen. We agreed on a fair rent. The house, which was within touching distance of the church, had perhaps 1,800 to 2,000 square feet. It had a dual outhouse with one half being for the congregation, and the other half being for the preacher and his family. The preacher's half remained locked and we promptly lost the key but gave them a combination lock, showing them how to use it. After we unpacked, I had Al or one of the interpreters keep an eye on the goods. I'd seen no sign of thievery in Haiti, but desperation pushes people beyond their normal habits. Just outside my bedroom door was a small laundry room, which Al & I converted into a shower room.

Almost immediately I announced that we had medicine and would be happy to try and help the sick. I believe in starting to dispense right away. The one thing I never want is to have a large stockpile of aid with the desperate having too much time to sit around and stare at it.

On the first night in Baie de Henne, the heat, flies, and mosquitoes were pretty bad. Early the next morning, before sick call, we went for a swim in the sea. Parts of the bottom were very rocky and other parts were filled with seaweed. Mud had formed a stable suspension in the water so there was no underwater visibility; it reminded me of Galveston. But unlike Galveston, Haiti has no continental shelf. The island of Hispaniola is the top of a mountain range. This meant that immediately beyond where the water met the beach, there could be considerable depth. It was strange to take the first step into the water and perhaps feel no bottom for your feet to rest upon.

I had taken a single waterbed that I might have a cool place to lay in the heat of the day, but I'd not considered how I would fill it. I had no garden hose as at home. Submerging it in the sea did nothing because of the equalization of pressure. Al suggested a funnel, which worked well enough to half fill the mattress before I finally gave up. The bed in my room already had partially collapsed springs and my weight, plus that of the water did them no good. The preacher would later demand compensation for his bed, but since it was junk from the beginning, he made good money off of us, and was already the richest man in town, I ignored that request.

On our second day in town there came a glorious downpour. The parched land had not seen rain in a long time, and one man said he thought we'd brought the town luck. As it poured off the metal roof of the preacher's house, I grabbed a bar of soap, and, dressed only in Bermuda shorts, had a cooling shower. Unlike in Yucatan, others followed me in doing so. Later when we would shower we would always use the army surplus canvas bag with the large showerhead on the bottom. Turning of the head to the left allowed the water to escape and turns to the right closed the valve.

I hired three men to begin digging a well in the coconut grove behind the main part of the village. I insisted on personally paying each worker each day to try and make sure he was a citizen of Baie de Henne and to keep a paymaster from assuming power he did not have. The water they were using was often polluted, and continual washing with salt water left their skin badly cracked. They were using some wells that were large, open and shallow, with ground contamination always present. My plan was to install a shallow well lift pump and have the area around the pump sealed. But I'd bought the finest screens I could buy for the pumps rather than buying an assortment of screens. The screens quickly plugged, preventing water from coming through the pumps. I hope that eventually someone diagnosed the problem and punched holes in the tight knit screen. It would have been preferable to have a little sand in the water rather than no water. Not understanding the problems, I had no alternative but to order the men to enlarge the well, using it as an open pit source of water. Still, the men enjoyed being paid for the work, stretched it out as long as possible and had better dipping water until it too became polluted. This was just one of many experiences I have had over the years which convinced me that third world missionaries should also have mechanical and agricultural skills. While living in Baie de Henne, life was not usually difficult. Yet I came down with the flu but had to walk to the farm some miles away to settle a dispute with the cooperative officials. When I returned, I had intended to cancel daily medical clinic, but Wesner informed me that 42 people had come from the mountains. They were particularly thin and had scales on their head from not washing. They had no soap and probably even had a hard time getting fresh water. There was also a high incidence of V.D. That was a very long day for me.

We had to hire a new cook and laundress. Our old one stole more than we could afford to lose to one person.

Kids would line up on the fence just outside the house all hours of the day. The interpreters would drive them off but they'd soon be back saying, "Mister, I am hungry. Mister, give me a quarter." For all I knew the interpreters might have taught them this. But requests for money constantly came in from some quarter. Even the preacher's wife asked for more money. The heat combined with the flu produced a little delirium in me but with my meds, I soon got the temperature down a bit and stayed in the shade for a couple of days letting Al assume many of my duties. Like me, in clinic he found that many people had large cracks in their skin from having to bathe with no soap, in salt water.

I would treat people medically for two hours each day and there would never be a shortage of people requesting medicine for this ailment or that injury. Al felt a little awkward treating, so I put him to doing the most basic of first aid. He would put iodine and dressing on cuts, and pass out bar soap with instructions for hygiene. As in Yucatan, when word got out there was aid available and free medicines, the cases grew more challenging. One man came to me with an arm looking as thought it needed to be amputated and I gave him a course of antibiotics and instructions to see the nurse I'd heard was in nearby Bombardopolis. A man came in with a terrible case of GC after I'd exhausted the antibiotics so I gave him money to also get to Bombardopolis. Mainly however, there were crowds of people with diarrhea, parasites, and malnutrition. Many also claimed 'Le Grepe', after the terrible influenzas of 1918. Some resembled old photos I'd seen of starving Biafrans from the civil war in Nigeria. To help dispense needed meds as quickly as possible I would give gallon cans of Kaopectate to a native, self-proclaimed Red Cross representative. She would return with requests for some more so quickly I began to wonder if they were not using it as a stomach filler like the Chinese eating mud soup in 'The Good Earth'. As a supplement to the food we gave, I dispersed liquid vitamins and V-8 in large amounts. While for speed sake I like to appoint others to help me with the dispensing of food and medicines, I like to also directly do so myself. It helps to insure that materials do not pool in the hands of a greedy few. I began by relying on the interpreters but I soon found that even though they were being paid, they were no more trustworthy than anyone else. Jeannot had a habit of pouring an entire can of cream meant for the children into his coffee. We had hired a woman to feed the four of us but I would often find Jeannot in the kitchen and I suspected he was telling her of his importance and that extra food for him would curry his favor. Other times, I would find him sitting in a chair like an Eastern Potentate while having a woman wash his feet and clip his toenails. I suspected that even his interpretations represented as much of his own ideas as mine and that he was making policy and greatly enjoyed appearing as a personal power. I feared he was making promises that neither he nor I could fulfill.

There was a fresh spring in town but it would spew out water from a embankment at sea level which made it difficult to separate from sea water or to use for bathing purposes.

The village was awash with children. By night when I was ready for bed, they would be hanging in the wood shuttered, unscreened windows of the house. By day there would be all sorts of children in the preacher's home and I never got straight on their parentage. I could not resist passing out little items here and there which really only served to increase their persistence. But we were not there to establish a children's program, but there rather to serve without regard to age or any other variable.

One frail woman came to see me from the mountains beyond. She was so tiny she reminded me of the Pigmies of Central Africa. She was one who was simply not equipped to compete in life. She was too tiny, too ignorant, too unskilled and too submissive. I marveled that this tiny, homely person had survived into what looked like her 30s. I gave her food, money, medicine and a blanket. Later, someone took the blanket from her. It is terrible what the depths of poverty can do to human beings. At its greatest depth you rarely find self-sacrifice. It is as though there is a crowd of people all dying of thirst when a small cloud suddenly releases a quart of water, which lands in a vessel. No one says "After you". One day I experienced, for the first time in my life, what true thirst was about. We had sailed to a nearby village on the coast to render some aid. I am not quite clear why I went, because I was keen on helping Baie de Henne and not diluting my resources in a futile effort to help the whole Northwest. Nevertheless, I went and we accomplished some good things. Upon preparing to leave, one of our helpers lifted our water barrel wrong and it fell, spilling all our drinking water. Under the hot sun we began to sail back. The ocean was shallow there and the bottom was covered with a thick coat of seaweed. The wind became too high for the boats so we were told we must walk.

So, we trudged to land and began to walk over the hills. By that time, even knowing the results would be catastrophic, I came within inches of drinking sea water. When we came to the first beach hut I emphatically ordered that drinking water be boiled immediately. While it was boiling, I ate 8 mangos for the juice. Once I had a total fast of 7 days in my youth. I knew starving to death would be an agony. Nevertheless, it would be vastly preferable to me, than to die of thirst. I'm certain I would very soon go mad. On that day I was quite happy to get back to the preacher's house. Enduring that level of thirst, I seemed unable to think about anyone other than myself. I was told by scuba divers that when the oxygen fails mothers will, in panic, grab the air from their children, and husbands from wives. The bottom line is that it becomes hard to blame people for their actions when lack presses hard enough.

CHAPTER 18

The local judge offered us his free land to do planting and wanted us to irrigate it from a source 4 miles away, but we were not there to improve an official's farm. He offered us some other land but said the water was 40 feet below. When we rejected this, he quickly revised his estimate and said the water was 8-10 feet below. Like everyone else, he tried hard to tell us what he thought we wanted to hear. He was not going to let the facts get in the way of a good story. I made it clear that the produce grown would be for all the people to share. They finally revealed they had a cooperative in operation. We then had a series of committee meetings regarding how everyone would share, and how workers who were not in the cooperative should be given a chance to work. I had taken care to select seeds that were not hybrids and could be saved from crops and replanted. While we still looked for suitable land to do planting, committees formed which I was expected to participate within, and the meetings droned on endlessly. I am a strong believer in democracy in the workplace, and that more heads are better than few even if it does require additional time. Too often the Japanese model has proven superior to the American model of management. The Japanese CEO does not make astronomically more than the company's workers. And they explain the program's aims and changes to every worker, soliciting complete agreement between management and worker. This takes time and usually ends up with the Japanese company starting behind the American company. But, since their work force is all on the same page, they quickly catch up and surpass us. Even at that, it was obvious that the Haitians were feeling their first taste of having a voice and were intoxicated by their participation. I wasn't interested in giving awards for pomp and fanfare. So, I would bear it as long as I could, and then would coax abbreviation, or leave altogether. The process had certain amount of seduction with it. Whenever I said something they wanted to hear, or would make a donation to something they had planned, they would give a round of applause. As time went by, they would sometimes get grandiose in their plans. They did not understand the difference between a lot of money and unlimited money. At one point they proposed that I pipe water from the mountains miles away to irrigate their land. I'm not good at estimating such projects, but I believe it would have taken $250,000 to get a good start. Even at that, only the government could get in enough PVC-pipe, which would quickly deteriorate in the harsh sun if not buried. They asked the logical question of how much money I had. I didn't answer; I could see no good use for that information. As it was they were very fond of arguing. When we finally found suitable land for us to farm, it was over two miles from our abode. We quickly agreed on a price, leaving me only to assemble the tools I'd bought and hire the workers. I hired about 20 men per day through a foreman. As far as I could tell, in Haiti, the foreman is exempt from any physical work himself – not a system I endorsed. But, I only insisted that the men hired be from Baie de Henne. I had paid $95.00 for the farmland to be used and had started a small garden nearby as well.

Since the sun came out early and hit hard, I assumed they would get an early start and come home earlier. This was not to be. Each day there would be 2 full hours of arguing before starting out for the farm. It wasn't just for the first few days it was every day. However, I figured that was their business until word reached me that the foreman was hiring men from other villages. I promptly put a stop to that. Matters went well for a while until one day a committee of women approached me stating that they wanted to work also. The men initially rejected the idea immediately. Even the pastor said "I work for Jesus Christ. The garden must be done right." I said, "That's good but women can work for Christ, too." The crowd laughed. In trying to gauge their objections (they had said women didn't know how to work) I said, "Women in China and Russia have long worked side by side with the men." The foreman, knowing nothing of either country, said, "That's different, their women are city women, ours are country women." I saw logic, and every book in a set of encyclopedias would not change their view, so I took another tack. I said, "I agree, your women do not know how to work, that is why you must teach them." This restored the pride of male superiority so they agreed. Henceforth, the work crew was to consist of 10 men and 10 women. The men had tendency to encroach on our agreement, and from time to time I had to intervene, but the ladies seemed quite pleased. This in no way solved the problem of morning bickering, however, it simply made the debates co-educational. It seemed to me that Haitians, in so many ways, are a people divided against themselves. Yet I doubt, given their poverty, it would be any different with any of us. It is sad, for there is little beyond people who are united, but when people are divided, so much energy is lost in internal squabbles.

We talked of the day when Al and I would leave, and one man asked, "When you go, who will tend the crops?" In a moment of frustration I said, "I'm not going to pay you to eat the crops." He agreed, he was simply making another pitch. It was a pitch gone wild, but it was worth a try. It was always curious to me that the workers were eager to go on to a new project before the last one was finished. I don't believe, for good reason, they saw success as tied to hard work.

Because walkers in the deep water could not use the seining nets I'd brought, the initial results were disappointing. I hired a fisherman to teach those who wanted to learn but did not know how. On the first use, he came in with only one fish, albeit one large enough to feed four people.

The Haitian fisherman showing his 1ˢᵗ catch with the nets I provided.

He said because the net was only six feet deep and could only be handled by boats, the fish would often swim underneath it. He asked permission to have the two three-hundred-foot nets sewn together. I informed him a net was one of the few things I'd promised to Pettit Paradise. He said they were part of the same fishing co-op so I gladly agreed. On Sunday, when I was in church, the fisherman showed up having caught about 30 fish with the combined nets. The town was abuzz. It wasn't the commercial size catch I'd hoped for from the nets, but it thrilled the people. And I didn't worry about someone hoarding the catch. The town had no ice, and on a hot day, fish can go bad in as short as one hour. So the rule was use it or lose it. I gave the church enough to feed a meal to the whole congregation since it was not fitting that worshippers should be the only ones without food. Control of the money was not always easy as someone would present me with fruit and then tell me a couple of days later I owed money for it.

Frequently the feared Ton-Ton would do practice marching. But the Ton-Tons of the countryside were very different from the thugs of Port-au-Prince. They were more like some home guard. When they would fall out for marching drill, it was comical. Some of the men would face left when ordered "right face" and they were all nice guys in tatters. Only one had a firearm, which looked like a rusty .38 revolver and I wondered if he had any ammunition for it. Certainly, he could not afford practice. Like so many others, he asked me for a big donation. I put him off. The head of the Ton-Tons was a handsome man of his late 20's. When our group would go sailing he liked to sing and had a beautiful voice. Under different circumstances, with a promoter, he could well have been another Harry Belafonte. On one of our first sailing trips he used the small motor I'd brought. It worked perfect for perhaps 100 yards, then began to sputter and stopped. It resisted restarting. Looking back, I believe I'd mixed far too much oil in the gasoline to keep the motor running. My mechanical expertise is nil. I gave it to someone who was very glad to receive it. He probably later made the opposite mistake and ran it without oil until it burnt out.

To solicit our favor, the town folk would often have some little gathering to honor us. And, as expected, I usually gave a small donation. They became more cheerful and participatory as I hired more of them. Once a youth club had a celebration with us as guests of honor. They played loud, Latin sounding music. I danced with Marie, a slender, light skinned girl with dimples that lived across the street and somewhat resembled Ava Gardner. Al danced with a girl they'd brought for his Terpsichore entertainment and that all seemed harmless enough. They served us some super sweet drink in tin cans wrapped in crepe paper, and gave us a small bouquet of flowers. I drank very little. Al must have enjoyed it as he drained his cup. That night, someone raced past my bed, and my first thought was that it was a thief. It turned out to be Al who barely reached the yard before he began to vomit. He must have puked for 15 minutes. I generally stayed healthy, but one day I got the flux so bad that as I was talking to the Ton-Ton leader I doubled over suddenly like I was on hinges, to keep from having an accident. I started walking very briskly after quickly excusing myself, only to be suddenly hit by another wave, which caused me to touch my toes. I barely made it inside the outhouse. The commandant may well have thought I used a ruse to avoid discussing his problem. His story was that he needed money for a new uniform or he would be in trouble with his supervisor. The girl across the street needed money or couldn't attend school (actually, I never saw a school). Everyone had their own problem.

When the preacher returned to his/our house after being gone for weeks, I found him to be the freest man in the village. He had been on his usual circuit. He traveled by horse to Gonaives and from there by car to Port-au-Prince. He was a short, generally friendly man who had the nicest house in town. Not being Baptist, I have no idea who supported him, but I felt certain he was getting funds beyond what his flock could provide. It appeared he was doing all his church overseeing as expected and had turned his ministry into a cottage industry. While others baked in the relentless sun of a community with no opportunities or anything of interest, the pastor, free of supervision, regularly went into Port-au-Prince and lived about as nice as one can without electricity.

At the opposite extreme in the village were the starving dogs. Being an animal lover, I fed them such as I could. At one point I suggested to the villagers that perhaps they should eat the dogs. A quick clean kill of the dogs would have been preferable to the slow torture of nature. But, they rejected the idea and I can't say it had a lot of appeal to me either. I have never been one to worry about catching anything from dogs. The only two things I am aware of that we can catch are ringworms (a fungus, not a worm) and rabies. Despite the lucrative business vets do giving rabies shots, I have only seen rabies once in my lifetime even living in the country surrounded by animals of all kinds. Dogs have a different anatomical system from humans, so there is little we can catch from them.

After we had been there a couple of weeks, Pastor Edgar came by to see how we were doing. It was comforting to have him in town since his was the only vehicle there. I told him I had spoken with a German attached to one of the welfare agencies and had confessed I had worried whether or not the authorities would allow me back into the Northwest on this second journey. He had laughed and said it didn't matter since in Haiti you could just help the first village you came to. Edgar agreed, but said he was happy we had come to the Northwest because no one else did. Certainly it was a desolate place.

While in the area we heard about a yacht wreck off the coast at Mole St. Nicholas. The story went that an early retiree from the New York City police department had married a Columbian exchange student and had two infant daughters. He was still young so the pair decided to realize a long time dream, buy a boat, and sail around the world. When they arrived off Mole, it developed a crack in the hydraulic steering system and began to slowly sink. They sent out mayday messages throughout the day never realizing there was not a receiving set in the entire Northwest. The Haitians, in a desperate attempt to earn some money, came aboard the sinking yacht trying to sell fish. Finally, the ex-policeman loaded his wife and children into a dingy and made for shore. Another nasty break came their way. The dingy capsized and while the pair managed to get themselves and their children ashore, their passports, and all their papers and stock certificates were lost. When in doubt, the rule of thumb in Haiti was to arrest. So, the Ton-Ton arrested the entire family. A CARE worker who happened to be present said, "That is ridiculous. If you arrest them, you must arrest me too." The order to arrest was vacated. The policeman, once ashore, sent a message to the American Embassy to send a car for him and his family. He was told, however, that rescuing wayward Americans was not their responsibility. In several spots in the world I have heard of the reluctance of American diplomats to do anything for our citizens having difficulties. Whatever the Embassies or Consulates do, they need to offer a public education program on their services and limitations. Again, Dr. Fougere came to the rescue, sending a car for the stranded family.

I had learned that, not too far away, there were some unfenced banana farms. I asked one of the citizens what would happen if someone was caught stealing bananas. He said the person would be quickly thrown into jail with no food and that he might be beaten or even killed.

Wesner announced at one point, he wanted to go to Port-au-Prince to give his family money. There had been no warning of this and I was glad I had hired two interpreters. Never the less, in the end he did not go. Possibly he felt we would not be there when he got back and that Jeannot would have gotten something he felt belonged to him.

Instead, we went to Pettit Anse to see if we could be of any assistance whatever. There we dug three wells, but predictably the water was useless. We first dug in a location villagers said that fresh water existed 50 years ago. We next dug near a tree that I can only guess must have been terribly salt water tolerant. We spent the night there and the mosquitoes were terrible. The following day, I saw 75 patients – giving medicine to all.

CHAPTER 19

Day by day, Al and I grew dirtier, more sun baked, and tired. This despite paying the preachers wife to clean our area, having our meals cooked for $20.00 a week, and paying a girl to do our laundry. Nevertheless our spreading around money kept the villager's spirits up, and our own, with the recognition we were doing something good. I also began giving away my personnel possessions such as my watch, a second pair of shoes, most of my clothing. Since it was obvious I was nearing the end of the project, I wanted to seize the opportunity to be of maximum use while I could. I had been in the village for one month. We did what we could to avoid disease. When I went to the toilet, Al would pour water for me to wash my hands and I would return the favor. It was considered perfectly acceptable to go behind a house to urinate. When I felt a little too close to having a heat stroke, I'd go inside and lay down.

As in Yucatan, the nights were filled with stars, far from the pollution and glare of the city. And the constant activity of the day made for good sleep at night even if the nights were warmer than ideal. It was good the weather was warm. Some of the children were naked and I did not see why many adults weren't. How they could get clothes replacements was a mystery to me. For there were no stores even if they had money.

A priest stationed in the town invited us by for "cocktails". He had no car, lived very poor and spoke only French. We drank something awful tasting and made a small contribution to his work. He was in Baie de Henne as a leprosy specialist from France. Our language barrier kept me from determining how long he'd been there and how successful he believed he had been. I am a Protestant, and yet I have an admiration for the Catholic clergy that take vows of poverty and live very humbly in terribly uncomfortable spots in the world. The Protestant efforts always seem to include trying to replicate middle class America. I understand that thinking tends to be clearer and plans more complete if one is not too hard pressed by environmental deficits. I suppose it boils down to how tough you are, and how determined you are to be one of the people rather than a benevolent overseer that they think they might become via a religious avenue.

A main problem that we encountered was the rivalry between interpreters. Jeannot came to me and told me that Wesner had been trying to get the town's officials to poison him. Further, Jeannot said that Wesner maintained I had promised him $20.00 per week rather than the $10.00 I was paying (on top of meals and lodging) and advised Jeannot not to work for less. Jeannot also indicated Wesner remarked that he was too good to talk to the poor people of the village. Clearly, Jeannot was making clumsy attempts to get me to move against Wesner. I told Jeannot that depreciating others seemed to be the national sport in Haiti, but I didn't want to become involved in such activities. That, at least, postponed their warfare.

Other clumsy attempts were made to influence me. When I explained how hard it was to get materials into the country, town people quickly offered to talk with a friend of President Duvalier and get me an appointment to speak directly with him. I suppose I was not as far from the Sunshine Grill as I'd thought. Chasing such wild rabbits would only detract from the work at hand. And everyday there were minor problems and many decisions to be made.

The day finally came when it was time to go back to Port-au-Prince. The money was spent and almost all of the materials were given out. Jeannot approached me with a direct accusation against Wesner. He said Wesner had been stealing things and a search of his bag and locker would reveal it. At my request, Wesner opened his bag and locker and sure enough there were items meant for the people. There were cans of food, flashlights and enough items to total perhaps $50.00. Wesner's excuse was that he had been promised a job for three months and we'd been in Baie de Henne for just over one month. Truthfully, I couldn't recall the exact words used when Wesner was hired. I may have given an estimate of longer than a month. But I was reasonably sure even if I had done so, I would have labeled it only an estimate. And, it was not as though Wesner had turned down another job to come with us. He left about $50.00 richer than when he came, (more than the weekly amount we had agreed upon) and had been well maintained while with us. I confiscated the stolen items amid Wesner's counter accusations against Jeannot, and sat on the porch to distribute them. As I sat on the porch distributing, the crowd became more and more grasping. Suddenly there were bodies and arms everywhere. I went into a fetal position to protect myself from the on rush. We found that some of the people had taken individual pump parts, which would be of no use to them. I asked for them back, but received no assistance. When I offered a dollar for each part they were quickly returned. I made arrangements for Pastor Shreeve to receive the extra pump. The commandant had offered to arrest Wesner, but I explained that I didn't want anyone arrested. Besides, Wesner was a scrawny guy who might not have survived jail. And, I had the philosophy that we all went to the Northwest and we all should come home. But to clear my head, I walked just out of town. Many of the town folk thought I was angry with them and followed me apologetically. The commandant, feeling the need to do something personal, made my bed and stayed nearby till I went to sleep, claiming they did not want me to sleep outside in rejection of the town. Actually, I wasn't even mad at Wesner, though I was sadly disappointed. I found out later the town folk were very angry at my interpreters for causing turmoil. They viewed our coming as an act of God and the first positive thing that had happened to their town in their memory. I had felt fine the first morning of distributing but even as I was distributing on the next and last day, a fever began to mount in me. Inside one and a half hours later, my temperature rose to 105 degrees. Thank God there was a jeep in town on that very day. Another priest had come by to visit the leprosy priest and agreed to take me to the hospital in Gonaives. It took three hours to get to the hospital, but seemed like thirty. As we bumped along the tropical road I began to vomit. Sometimes I could get my head outside the window in time, sometimes not. The kindly priest, also from France, checked me into the hospital there in the area of famine. The hospital there had a doctor who spoke almost no English. He did say, "You can tell me all your problems". But I saw no need to remain there for life. It was run by the Catholics and was the kind of hospital I would like to die in. There was a real shower and toilet down the hall. Outside my room was a well-kept garden atrium with flowers in abundance. It was all at ground level with no doors on the outside rooms. It was clean and neat, but not sterile. A dog wandered into my room and even in my delirium I benefited from hanging my arm off the bed and petting him briefly. I could only eat a little bread and drink a little juice. They put me on something intravenously and hired a pretty nurse to watch me around the clock. She spoke no English and performed no known service. She only sat and watched. I suppose if I'd begun thrashing or yelling she would have alerted the doctor. The following day I was served a typical American breakfast and checked out feeling much better. My total hospital bill was $64.00. Later an official with AID said he thought I'd had Dengue Fever as it was very prevalent in that area. I have no idea how the interpreters returned to Port-au-Prince but I'm sure they managed quite well.

When we went to Port-au-Prince, it was with a small girl who had been so stricken with polio that her effected leg was notably shorter than the other. In fact to stand, she had to kneel with the normal leg while she stood with the short leg. I checked her into another Catholic hospital with a plea that they do whatever they could for her. I offered to pay, but the good sister simply scooped the little girl into her arms and said, "We'll take care of her." If I'd ever had reservations about the work, the trip, they were shredded at that moment.

When we got back to the Sendral Guest House, I was introduced to the new guests. Upon meeting a man about 42 years of age I said, "Oh yes, Jack, you're the one whose yacht sank." He clammed up immediately. I was told he was quite nervous about the incident and only wanted to get his wife and children out of Haiti as quickly as possible. He had told no one in Port-au-Prince about his arrest and thought I might be CIA and willing to entangle him in a situation. I didn't try to get any information from him, and only felt sorry for his misfortune. Looking back, I believe one thing that Haitian villages badly need is a holding tank so that they can chlorinate their water. We observed in Haiti that the Americans, as a group, were very critical of the Haitians. Their accusations were that the Haitians are lazy, won't work even for their own interests, steal and live on a system of corruption and graft. It seems unrealistic to me to have middle class expectations of people who have suffered so greatly, and for whom hard work has never paid a suitable dividend. Doubtless, many Haitians have learned some undesirable, dysfunctional patterns of behavior. Yet behaviors are learned and new patterns can be developed. I'm not saying I could develop them or that it would be easy, yet to paraphrase Luc Nere, "As long as you call the people lazy and the situation hopeless, you'll never cure it". I seriously doubt that, given their meager meals, non-Haitians would present a superior model of energy and motivation. Once back from Baie de Henne, Al and I spent the little time before our flight to Houston living as cheaply as possible. I arrived back in Houston with a credit card and 78 cents in my pocket, and a plan to take Linda to Afganistan. But that, as they say, is another story.

Years later, I took scuba lessons and tried to interest someone in going to Mole St. Nicholas with me and diving for the sunken boat. It was barely off shore and the entire town knew its sunken location. It was fiberglass in construction. I was told that after a few years in the salty water it would not be worth salvaging. I'm sure the insurance company decided it might as well be on the dark side of the moon. I thought with enough rope I could hire the whole town to try and pull it ashore. Once ashore, it might be possible to make minor repairs and have myself a yacht. I couldn't interest anyone into going with me however, so I finally went alone. But on this, my last trip to Haiti, I was without charity credentials and found the cost for getting to the Northwest prohibitive to say nothing of other expenses involved in such an operation. And, even had I made it to Mole, the boat may be hung on an underwater cliff in a delicate state of balance like the Red Witch, or it may have fallen into a deep crevasse. Too, I had wanted to go to the Northwest to find what had happened with the crops and if the people were any better off. In the end, I had to settle for the knowledge that I came with thousands of dollars and at least eased the pain for a while. And a while is all we can ever guarantee.

CHAPTER 20

India

Tales of lives beyond ordinary controls have been a corkscrew to my own. A short, incomplete, but intriguing story was told to me on a long, dull Texas afternoon. It was the kind of day that made time and events seem forever the same. So perhaps it would not have sounded strange on some New Year's Eve at Mardi Gras. The story came to me from a management employee of an international chemical company. It seems that one of his fellow employees, stationed at a branch plant in India, took a fancy to an "untouchable" in her late teens. Though the plant worker was middle aged, he invited the girl to share his bed, board, and body. She saw the invitation as a way to scale the survival ladder, and he became something of a Professor Higgins with sexual overtones. In cohabiting, he had to instruct the girl on western standards of hygiene and diet. This probably was not a quick, simple matter. Typically, Indians practice ablution rather than using toilet paper, and it is very unlikely that kissing was a part of her culture. Then there were such things as how to eat with utensils, how to clean teeth with a toothbrush rather than a roughened twig, and how to use a western toilet. The plant worker was largely condemned by his fellow employees and their families for taking the girl in "just so he could sleep with her." Still, he was undaunted by their criticisms. He freely admitted he slept with her. Nevertheless, he contended he did not have to take her into his quarters merely for that purpose. For there was no shortage of bed partners in India for one seeking only sex. And it must be conceded that not all satyrs are evil in their entirety. Even so, local prejudices had infected the Americans, and their rejection of the young harijan was complete. When she would go into the company swimming pool, the Americans would come out. As I listened to the story, I thought the girl must have been very beautiful for employee's wives to put that much energy into their rejection. It seems highly unlikely that solid company men would leave their wives in search of their own comely street girl. There would, after all, come a day of reckoning for wayward married men. Yet sometimes all it takes is one deviation from the pattern to send ripples of anxiety through a crowd of women who see their core role as having once been decorative.

When the man's contract in India was concluded, he returned to the U.S. without the young woman. Thankfully, he left her with no children, and had helped her attain a place in a strata of Indian society, albeit a humble one. He had secured a job for her in a local brick factory. If the wages were meager, the work was steady, and she was self supporting for the first time in her life. She need never be under some husband's thumb unless she so chose. The man died some years later without ever detailing or recording his adventure. Such a pity that there are so many unanswered questions. Oddly, I wondered if Crest is still making money on her or did she return to using a twig for dental care? Did she believe she had benefited from their arrangement, or did she feel used and poorly rewarded? Was she able to bag a husband, or was she considered tainted among her own crowd? Did he ever meet her family, and if so, what was their reaction? Did he consider marrying her, and if not, why not? When he left did she dissolve into salty tears, or was she somewhat glad to see him go? These are questions that will never be answered. I particularly enjoyed the tale because of its breaking free of convention. I would not recommend its re-enactment. It was a quick and dirty way of bridging two cultures. Even so, people who spike my interest are those who dance to music that they alone hear, and in doing so increase the combinations available to us all. In life's beginning, everyone wants to fit in. And exploring new paths is generally done by those who have first been rejected by the standard, old ones. So many come to later recognize a great debt to that rejection. At day's end, the only rejection you have to fear is self-rejection. Self-rejection paves an avenue that leads to alcoholism, depression, and drug use.

To me India is the most heterogeneous, and for that reason, the most interesting, country on earth. The extreme variety does not always make for a pleasant experience, just a varied one. Each family even has its own curry recipe and I can testify I've never had bad chicken curry in India. The very lengthy history of India coupled with the numerous castes and sub castes leave a westerner befuddled. Add to that the greatly different topography of the subcontinent and you're bound to find things you like. Actually, I suspect that people that don't both love and hate India know little of the country. Whether you love mountains, or the desert, jungle or the city, India has it. And to have so many people, due to the power of the family, India can be a very prudish country.

A vivid memory I have is taking the Rajdhani Express from Howrah station in Calcutta, to New Delhi (1443 kilometers), an overnight trip. I still smile when I look at the ticket I kept for a souvenir. The station was only moderately busy, but luggage was weighed rather than measured. And in my experience when Indians travel, they take everything but their plumbing with them. The ticket advertised "air conditioned sleeper". It proclaimed "Indian Railways welcome you aboard the Rajdhani Express. Evening tea, dinner, morning tea and breakfast will be served to you during the journey." Being somewhat clumsy at buying the ticket, I was assigned an upper berth in a sleeper with 3 Indian gentlemen. We immediately set out to get to know one another. One was angry at the difficulty involved in getting into America for a visit. But generally, the conversation was quite amiable. I noticed one giving his attention to a magazine I had picked out which was the Indian equivalent of "Photoplay" featuring an attractive Indian film star on the cover. As I'd already read it, I offered it to him. He said, "Oh, no, my wife would think I had fallen in love with the actress." In the long night we compared cultures and had a very pleasurable trip. I hated for it to end.

I've always felt safe in India. The most dangerous thing I've encountered there was in the Calcutta Museum. A crocodile some fourteen to sixteen feet long had eaten enough people, as evidenced by bracelets, anklets, etc. to account for devouring more than a dozen. Yet since the dead are sometimes placed in the Ganges, one wonders if they were alive when he ate them. As I stood on the banks of the Ganges, a tall Sheik from South Africa, seeing his home country for perhaps the first time, stated with gestures, "I would not even put my little finger in the Ganges, yet two days ago I saw a man plunge beneath the depths, come up with a mouthful, and gargle mind you."

Upon renting a car and a driver we drove past a grassy esplanade where I noticed a holy man, and something to my casual glance appeared different about him, but we were too quickly gone to deliberate what. On our return at the end of the day, the man was still there and suddenly it struck me. He was totally naked. His body was covered with ash but he wore nothing and I seemed to be the only one who noticed.

By the time I set my village quest on this other half of the world, I was slowing down and felt over confident on addressing the problems of tropical villages. I had been to India a couple of times previously, had compared notes with a former Peace Corp volunteer, and believed I knew all I needed to know until I had selected a village. But the subcontinent is a huge place, far larger than Yucatan and Haiti put together. A coworker of mine was from the state of Gujarat, just north of what was still called Bombay at the time. He begged me to consider Kashmir though he had never actually been there. Stories that he had heard made it sound like Paradise but quite poor. I knew that the British, in former times, had gone to Srinagar, its capital, on holidays to escape the oppressive heat. What little I read on it made the houseboats on Dal Lake sound wonderful. And if I could go out, work by day and then repose in comfort by night, I thought it would be good. I had some mild reservations about it being a Moslem area. As a group, the Moslems seem contentious to me, and I generally found theirs a fairly joyless culture. But human beings, after all, have more in common than we have differences. So I agreed to go to Srinagar to begin my search. Armed with my own money and about $750.00 given to me by a godly woman, Ida Sing, a widowed old friend of the family, I undertook the long journey to the other side of the world. A travel agency had misinformed me that I could get my visa in India. En route I was to find this was false. Requirements stated that you must obtain your visa in your home country unless a letter accompanied your application from the U.S. Consulate requesting that you be given a visa. By the time I got to Hong Kong, I approached the U.S. Consul who was reluctant to give me a visa request letter because Indira Gandhi had just been assassinated, and disturbances were expected. However, with proper pleading, I was given the letter and subsequently received a visa from the Indian Consulate.

When I arrived in India I personally saw no problem with disturbances, but I felt a little strange taking the long flight to Srinagar. There was only one other Anglo booked on the flight. She was an Irish woman whose family had immigrated to Australia. She had been sent by the High Commission to determine if another Australian woman had remained in Kashmir by her own choice, or if she had been coerced against her will. The woman had been gone for some years, and her family was concerned about her. While I understood their concern, it seemed a bit late in the game to be doing such an investigation. But then I know little of the details of the situation – only that she had been one of the "Flower Children" drifting around the world in search of meaning and method. I supposed she must have written her family at one time for them to even know where she was. The Irish lady even had directions to the house where the former Flower Child could be located.

Irish seemed particularly glad that there was another westerner on the plane, and immediately struck up a conversation. Following some sort of herd instinct, we agreed to take our perspective rooms on the same houseboat.

As we arrived, there were numerous houseboat owners making pitches and I allowed her to select our new residence. We were taken by one of the skiffs out to the houseboat that was offshore but connected to the mainland by a waterline. In post-colonial times, British officials had been replaced as residents by hippies who liked to use hashish and swim nude, while partying, to the shock of the Kashmiris. But we had arrived in October and the other houseboats were without customers. Since the area was in an on-going dispute between Pakistan and India, it was not deemed the safest place to go.

We were immediately each given a room and introduced to the chef. He was a young, handsome lad with the uniform and tall stovepipe hat of a chef. My room was comfortable with a large layer of blankets and a large bathtub with hot water on demand. It had windows through which a boarder could yell (or enter if you allowed it), "Please sir, I want to be your tailor", or "Chocolate, hashish?"

But, besides there being very few people on the street or on Lake Dal Lake, something else was wrong. The houseboat was drafty and a chill came in through the crevices. Wasn't India supposed to be a hot country? What was this chill I was feeling? We were in a valley at the foot of the lesser Himalayas (the "Hindu-Kush" or "Hindu Killer" mountains).

The day after I arrived it snowed! Then I recognized all too well that in not doing my homework, I'd made a very serious mistake. Kashmir would not be able to grow anything until the following spring. Mine could be a charity mission, one to demonstrate to the local population that not all westerners were shocking in their behavior, or uncaring toward Moslem agony. It just could not be a full village project. The reconnaissance and the project would be one in the same. I only had a month off from my vacation and didn't have the resources to fly south and begin the search for a more appropriate village. And a large part of what I sought was a third comparison of cultures.

There was one Christian church in town, but unlike the Mosques that seemed to always be open, it was closed except during services. I found one physician, but the Moslem doctor's office was small and covered with dust. I was reluctant to patronize it.

There was one luxury hotel just outside of town; I believe it was the Obregon. Irish and I ate supper there once and inquired about the price of their rooms. The rooms were expensive and I told them so. I asked if they were willing to cut the rate since it was obviously off-season. They replied "No", that such would compromise them as a deluxe hotel. I thought this bizarre since, as far as we could tell, the hotel had no guests, and no one else was eating in the large dining room. There was plenty of staff, but the service was slow.

We each bought a heavy woolen caftan to ward off the chill, and went to an area where many crafts booths had been established for the tourists that were nowhere to be found. I don't think I've ever seen such bored expressions as those on the faces of workers manning the booths. They were apparently paid by the government, though with no training or interest in hawking their goods.

I made the best deal I could on the black market in transferring dollars into rupees. Unlike Mexico where they want their paper only intact and without rips or defacements of any kind, the rupees had a hole punched through them for bundling with string. My interpreter (and chef) carefully explained to the moneychanger that I was there to give money to the poor, not as a merchant. He finally gave me a good rate, and I had a large stack of 100 rupee notes. With driver and chef, we began going to poverty pockets and distributing. At one point the push for money became so intense that he shoved me into the car and we sped away as outreached hands grabbed for us. Usually, however, the reaction, while grateful, was not so frantic. We gave money for seeds, for food, and for medical treatment. We passed a large Mosque with people stretching their hands heavenward for such as they hoped God would provide.

Lights in the town were only on for several hours per night and by candlelight a host of errors could be concealed in the food. I ate at a Tibetan restaurant one night and soon after grew ill. For about 2 days I felt blue green, lying in my bed with Irish expressing worry over me, and asking the houseboat owner to take care of me. Still, I would not go to the one doctor's office I previously mentioned. After about two days it felt as though a lunch I'd had ten years ago was coming up on me. I ran towards the bathroom but only made it as far as the metal waste can. I vomited for what seemed like an eternity but afterwards, felt good. Needless to say I did not return to that restaurant.

I wanted to push on to Leh and Ladakh but the mountain passes fill with snow and could not be traveled. Those spots, on the Tibetan Plateau are probably more Tibetan than Tibet itself since the Chinese have absorbed the region.

We soon made contact with the woman that Irish had been sent there to check on. She and her husband lived right on the shore of Dal Lake. She was washing clothes by hand in the lake and had a couple of infants in tow. She invited us for tea and while she was not loquacious, she talked enough to leave no doubt but that she was married and planned to stay. Her home surpassed the stick huts of Yucatan, and the tin and cloth shelters of Haiti, but not by much. Why any woman would leave the comforts of modern Australia for a life of no luxuries on Dal Lake mystified me. But it wasn't my business, so Irish and I left with her word that she would write the family and send pictures. She was definitely a woman that marched to a different drummer. In driving through the countryside, we visited one very pretty young widow whose husband was, I think, lost in the conflict with India. Her future seemed very uncertain. My driver told me there it is difficult to marry a Muslim woman.

When I left Srinagar and its surrounding villages, the airport security man said, "My job is very boring, next time, bring a bomb." I'd had a ring maker make a very large ring for me out of silver, he said "Good for fighting." There was too little to compare the cultures of Kashmir with Yucatan and Haiti as regards propensity for self-help, but the Kashmiris seem to have been far more impacted by the violence of the area. They were far more seeped in religion and more willing to see violence as having a part in life. Of course it was all in defense of land, defense of money, defense of family. In defense of the characteristics of the people of that area, I believe the area should have gone to Pakistan, not India, when England divided the two countries. The population is Moslem, and was at the time of the partition. Through some process, at the time Pakistan and India were separated, the region was ruled by a Hindu Maharajah. The British gave him the choice to go to Pakistan or India, and after much vacillation, he chose India. India promised a plebiscite, but it is a promise unfulfilled.

The following year I received a Christmas card from the chef, which I thought was a very nice thing to do. After all Christmas is a Christian celebration, and the card took a bit of money and time. I had, of course, given him a generous tip at journey's end. I felt fatherly enough to him to want to marry him to some U.S. girl where upon he could live a better life. But that is a very complex, costly procedure. I left India, as I had Haiti, moderately determined not to return but rather to concentrate any future efforts on Villa Linda de Yaxachen. I was out of villages, out of strength and determination, and out of the conviction that I could bring social justice to the whole world. Yet I had done much more then, in my rational moments, I thought I could, and had attained a level of peace that I could never have found before the village work. My life had meant something. If I never go to another village it will be O.K. because in some corridor of time, I am still there. Perhaps I am just outside a Mayan hut having chicken soup with the town's mayor, sometimes I'm laughing with a road worker who has a problem because he and I both know I can and will fix it. Then I may be swimming on the coast of Haiti with a beach all to myself. I have such a collection of memories that I could have never equaled by just staying home, joining the country club, or working my way up the corporate ladder. I did something for God; He did more for me.

Recommended for Anyone Interested in Adopting a Village

Being aware that people usually do not use advice they have not asked for, I will keep mine at a minimum.

1. Select a village as far from central governmental authorities as possible. That is one of the things I did right. I doubtless saved my volunteers, the villagers, and myself, much harassment and attempts to extract bribes. Minimize any communication with the government. I never tell their government of any plans nor try to get their permission for our activities. Yet often only the capital sells more basic necessities. Keep that in mind as regards spare parts or special tools you may need.

2. Unless you are very at home in the 3rd world, at least one reconnaissance trip is essential. Take a notebook and make good notes of your questions, observations, and experiences. Meet every worker there you can, taking their identification data for future contacts. Liberate a phone book from your hotel in the large city you fly into so you can later determine resources in the area. Note modes of cheap transportation.

3. Take all promises from natives of the country to help you, with more than a grain of salt. I have found they are almost always empty promises.

4. Make sure you have ample interpreters if you do not speak the language fluently. Communications are slow, particularly if several people need an interpreter at once. Too, more than one interpreter can serve as a safeguard against interpretation errors, either accidentally, or because the interpreter has his own agenda. Interpreters recommended by clergy are probably safest.

5. In dispersing money, when possible, have them work for the money on some project that will help the village. In that way,

everyone benefits. This way too avoids building any sense of entitlement and preserves dignity (though I have never found that a problem).

6. Be slow to promise but consistent in delivery of whatever you do promise. I never use the word "try". It is an escape hatch word. It is a child's way of raking in early credit or gratitude without actually having done anything. I have personally found that when people say, "I'll try," it never happens. The best builder of admiration, and your best safeguard, is to look and act responsibly.

7. If the country you have selected is especially poor and you are going into a remote area, let the U.S. consulate know where you are going. There is often a registry to sign. Collect whatever written information they have on the country. Sometimes they have a list of approved doctors, various disease rates, and other valuable statistics.

8. Read whatever is available on the area you pick. The U.S. Government Printing Office puts out area handbooks on countries of the world, and Washington has phone warnings for areas considered unsafe to travel within. Above all, learn when the rains come and go, as crops must be planted in conjunction with the rainy season. Time your arrival with their rainy season. There will be no irrigation and there must be rain for your plants to grow. In the tropics, the "winter" months have no threat of freezing.

9. Know that you will generally have no problems accumulating prescription medicines. Most poor countries do not require a prescription. They are readily available in their pharmacies or pharmaceutic houses. Slightly out of date meds are fine usually. I've mainly used Lomotil for diarrhea, antibiotics, water purification tablets or chlorox, decongestants, antiseptics, and worm medicine. Do some first aid studies.

10. Have your entire plan, and alternatives, in your head. Do not leave key sections of the plan to someone else for the sake of specialization. Too often people simply do not keep their

agreements and will sometimes back out at the last minute. Depend on no one but yourself.

11. Take dried foods that do not have to be cooked. For foods that have to be cooked, hire a village woman to do so. She needs the money and you need the time.

12. Figure that clean water will be a problem wherever you go. Have means of purifying what you drink. It is probably a safe assumption there will be parasites, and respiratory problems during the rainy season.

13. Do not go alone but minimize the ones you take along. The villagers can supply all the clever labor you will need. If you went alone it would be well except you might need someone to help you get medical help. And you have to have a stomach for loneliness. I would take a unisex group if I were to take a group at all.

14. Do not micromanage the villagers. Give them the idea of what you want done and stay out of their hair. When you are around them doing some work, pitch in.

15. Take precautions against illness. A sudden illness at the wrong time can make the whole project go down the drain. Prior to the trip, get in the best physical condition you can. Everything is easier if you're fit.

16. Take lots of cash in small units. I have never found a place you could not pay in U.S. dollars, but there is never change available.

17. Take as much with you as you can get into the country or on the plane but plan on buying any bulk food or specialized items there. I have taken many things I have never used. The only things you can be sure will be put in to use are food, medicine, and clothes (light for the tropics).

18. When you have selected your village, spot the location nearest you of a mechanic, any medical facility, and any bus route. You may never need them but you'll feel less vulnerable knowing where they are.

19. If you rent a car in the capital, don't reveal your destination. Car agencies expect their cars to travel down more or less standard roads, not to be taken into jungle, no road terrain.

20. Learn as many words of their language as you have the heart to. One of our first words in Spanish was 'necessito' (I need). To that I could add many nouns and verbs.

21. Villagers often have some superstitious, child-like beliefs. I give them my honest opinion. Sometimes they believe me, sometimes they go right on believing what they formerly believed. I've never seen them resent the expression of my opinion.

22. It is important to be polite to the villagers, but never be afraid to be directive or to hurry them if circumstances require it.

23. If you have in mind several programs within the village, you might start them simultaneously, support the ones that are most supported by the villagers and let the others collapse. Give yourself permission to make a mistake.

24. In the village you will be staying in someone's house. Pay them rent either with money or extra food and gifts. Whether your projects will really help the village remains to be seen. I have never seen a villager refuse money or gifts. They know you've got it, and they know that they need it.

25. If at all possible, have access to some vehicle during your stay in the village in case you need prompt medical care.

26. You will probably be the most important person to ever pay attention to their misery. I've never had a villager refuse a request, though I have had occasion where my instructions were not carried out as I had intended and supervision was needed.

27. Take along lots of tiny paper cups to disperse medicine for the villagers.

28. It is a myth that people will only eat their traditional foods. Sometimes that is because they have no choice. When I have given them the choice, I have found them at least as adventuresome as Americans in trying new foods.

29. Be prepared to slow-go in almost everything. Often, villagers are more time aligned to the seasons than the hour, and even those in the capital will not feel your sense of urgency.

30. In villages most of the people are related so to help one often results in helping others. But there seems to be very few boundaries and no privacy. Their family structure and distribution of what they receive is often incomprehensible to the new outsider. Strife becomes more pronounced as the villages get larger. I would always target the smallest village possible.

31. If you resent sweating, lack the patience to tolerate some slowness and inefficiency, and cannot abide riding in the back of a fruit truck or similar transport, don't go.

32. Most importantly, stick close to God. His schedule and method, even His goals, may be quite different from your own, but in the end He'll make things work out for the best in my experience.

33. Know that you may never be able to take a third world vacation again. If you are not haunted by gaunt, hungry faces then you will, at the very least, have a new knowledge of the lives of those serving you.

34. I'm not going to say it is impossible to get into trouble, but if you avoid politics, show some effectiveness in helping and avoid getting embroiled in personal squabbles, you will probably be far safer than walking the streets of Los Angeles. There is a great social barrier between you and the locals that few of them would take a chance in fracturing. It might incur the wrath of other villagers or even the authorities who have horrific jails for their own citizens.

35. When you finish your project, it will probably feel like the most meaningful thing you've ever done, and may hook you for life. And it's very soothing to feel like you've really made a difference – not just to family and friends – but to an entire village.

36. As the reader is doubtless able to tell, I am an adult Christian, not a sugar plumb prince Christian. If you are afraid of words,

or recoil at some of the things people may do to survive in the third world, you're probably better off staying at home and financially supporting those with a little more grit who do go.

37. In my prayers, I solicit God's help in getting as many people as possible to leave comfort of hearth and home to go and touch remote areas. I encourage readers to ask themselves, "If you don't go, who will?" And I equally pray that you come home when you are ready to do so with even less illnesses that my own.

EPILOGUE

My hope had always been that others would be inspired to adopt a village upon considering what an educational adventure it is. My hope also is that it not be merely educational, but life fulfilling and God pleasing. There were many people that went with me over the years, particularly to nearby Mexico, but almost all went once, filed the experience away, and went on with their ordinary lives. One young lady had said, "This is what I want to do with my life", but she did something else. There was an exception, a writer named Steve Brigham who did so very much, and went for years. Yet outside of Linda, who aided me in the work from the beginning, the one person who never quit was Diane Melson Haws. The work of this slight girl has been all the more impressive, as she has been legally blind from an early age from Macular Degeneration. As far as I am able to determine, she never allowed this disability to stand in her way whether she went alone or guided others. She alone was responsible for getting a team of optometrists from the University of Houston School of Optometry to go to the village. They took with them 300 sets of eyeglasses and gave eye exams to most of the folk there. To those who fear going to an unknown village might result in their being killed, maimed, or robbed, I say look to Diane. Each time she went, she would give me a wonderful report of their progress. I recall her first telling me electricity had come to Yaxachen. It meant that as the gasoline pump was about to fail, I could get them a far cheaper, more practical, submersible pump.

None of the changes in the village were more dramatic than those reported in her September trip of 2007. She saw a few cars and several modern houses. The village had grown from the original 400 to about 1,200 in population. Much of the improvement is the result of about 150 of the young men working in the U.S. and sending money home. The elementary school that formerly had trouble keeping one government teacher now has a dozen teachers, and there are five teachers in their middle school. Children wanting a high school education can achieve it on a computer there.

My frequent trips to the village for many years may have triggered a recognition that the vast land to the north offered opportunities to plug into. Legal or illegal, I have never found it in me to blame the ultra poor for going where work is available to feed themselves and their children. And some have neither the mechanism nor the time to come through legally. They will not sit in a corner and politely starve to death to satisfy philosophical positions of their northern neighbors.

My only angst has been the poor of Mexico having so many children. Unchecked population will, in time, make the U.S. another Mexico. Then Canada would be next in the firing line. But perhaps Mexico City, being the largest on earth, with approximately 25 million, has skewed my vision. I am one who worries about world population as we crowd out other species and produce global warming. Surely I don't need to say there is a difference between birth control and starving those who are already here. On one trip I had a nurse give a talk to the villagers on the rhythm method. As I have said, it was chiefly attended by men.

I had what might be my last trip late in 2008. I don't know if I will make it to the village again. I no longer walk very well or far, and I ache from stern to aft. But it doesn't really matter if I do or don't. God has answered my prayers for the village beyond my dreams. I send money to little Delmi and my old village friend Feliciano, and that is not such a bad second place to actually going.

Today I live with Linda in thickly wooded acres in the rolling hills of beautiful, but often hot, East Texas. We share our house with a live-in Hispanic handyman, 13 dogs and many cats. As God is a different species from us, yet calls us His children, so it is between us and our devoted furry kids. I feed the wild animals, also, who croak, chatter, and call me "father" in unknown tongues.

A creek runs through our property named "Sandy Creek" which was my nickname as a boy. It is as though I was meant to be here.

From my days as an Eagle Scout I learned to be awed by nature. I know it can be cruel, but it sustains so many, and its beauty cannot be denied. I gaze out my window at the woods wherein every tree and leaf is a little different from every other one. Small wonder Van Gogh said, "Christ is a greater artist than all other artists". I am old now, and somewhat broken, but I feel a great contentment that I once did something that truly mattered to myself, my family, and to so many others. It seemed to make up for so many things I've done, or neglected to do.

I grew up as an only child in a blue-collar neighborhood in Houston. I spent so many of my school years day dreaming and looking out the window instead of being focused on studies. I discovered 'C's were the best grade I could get for the effort. Even 'B's required some work. By the 8th grade I begged my parents to let me drop school. My secret plan was to go to Mexico and seek my destiny. Little did I know Mexico would house much of my destiny, but not for many years to come. Despite enlisting the endorsement of our neighbor, a former racecar driver, my parents solidly nixed my plan. Thank God. Yet by high school I was spending even more time gazing out the window. I could see men working on the road with an air hammer and how I wished I could be one of them – anything but a student at Milby High. Milby was not a blackboard jungle school but it wasn't a prep school either. Social cliques and a system that rewarded rebellion more than scholarship, left most of us who were neither members of the in-crowd or award winners, feeling like strangers in a strange land.

While day dreaming, I failed algebra and mechanical drawing. However, after doing make-up in summer school, I was told by the school counselor I could graduate a semester early if I wished. I jumped at the chance. But with my birthday falling at the beginning of September, I was already the youngest in our class. The skipped low senior year put me in a homeroom with even older students. One or two had a 5 o'clock shadow, and one or two were going bald. I explained to the new homeroom students that I had failed and was being put back. They accepted this. It was better to me that they think I was a bit on the dumb side than young as I was. So, I missed the "egghead" label despite the fact that years later, in the army, I only had to shave every other day. But when I got out of high school I had no plan whatever. All my conscious life I'd been in school. Now, suddenly that was over. I awoke the morning after graduation with a freedom hangover. As my dad had always been of the ilk that boys were either in school or hitting the bricks for a job, I was expected to find employment. And the jobs available for the 17 year old with no skills, no credentials, and no experience, were a grim prospect indeed. But somehow, precisely how lost in the corridors of time, I landed a job with a large distributing company that normally was known for hiring winos to put circulars of grocery specials on house doors. This special contract paid twice the normal amount and we carried cases of soap on our backs putting a new bar of Zest on the door of much of Houston.

I've learned in my contact with manual laborers over the years that they are not stupid, as I once would have assumed. Mainly, they are odd shaped pegs that do not fit within the holes society has carved out. Their problem is one more of emotions than intellect. On one such job my co-worker was a likeable lad but who had an authority problem. Each time a boss would be verbally abusive, he would give the boss five knuckles across the mouth. This resulted in a downward spiral in his career, which made him more likely to encounter a verbally abusive boss. Yet another co-worker claimed he had a massive string of speeding and parking tickets unresolved, and that he stayed one step ahead of arrest warrants. Some enjoyed day work for its flexible tolerance of whether they showed up for assignment on a given day. Two young men, of the same size, after working hard all day, would spend as little as possible on their room and peanut butter crackers, saving the bulk for prolonged beer busts. When they finally staggered home, they would peel off their clothes, fling them in the corner and be asleep as soon as they hit the mattress. The next morning, pre-dawn, they would, in the dark, put on whatever clothes they first reached from the pile in the corner and repeat the day before. Their story sounded like something out of Orwell's "Down and Out in Paris and London".

But while distributing soap, I met a 35-year-old Mexican-American named Ralph who liked to honky-tonk but had no car. As a green 17 year old, I wanted to serve an apprenticeship in honky-tonking, and I had a car. Ours was a symbiotic match. Ralph liked to drink, but mainly he was looking for a cheap, easy tryst. He was very equalitarian in his choice of women – young, old, pretty or ugly, it was all the same to Ralph. He was a laborer by day, a satyr by night. Maybe he was just looking for a way to numb the pains and disappointments he suffered by day. While playing chauffeur on Ralph's nightly rounds, he introduced me to a cute, 22 year-old name Lupe. Lupe and I became an instant item. She was a "Taxi dancer". For the reader who may not be familiar with the term, a taxi dancer was a girl who danced with any man who asked and paid 25 cents. The system was identical to the girls of New York of the 30's which made famous the song "Ten Cents a Dance". But no tickets were purchased in the Mexican cabarets; it was strictly cash and carry. Most of the girls were part time prostitutes and used the dance as an opportunity to talk terms to the patrons - Mexican laborers. Men who work hard often play hard as well. Lupe and I parted company when, after a drinking bout, she was in a car accident requiring lengthy hospitalization for a broken leg. Nevertheless, when dad heard I was going with a taxi dancer, it went down badly. And, when I told him it was my intention to join the army, and go to Germany, it was instantly seen as a sign that my trajectory was far off course. He offered me a trip to Europe or Africa, knowing I dreamed of world travel, if I would forgo the army for 2 years of college. I was given 2 hours to consider his offer. A quick look at a world map showed I'd either have to go through Europe to get to Africa or take weeks by ship. Besides, I had distant relatives living in Africa. Only one thing stood in my way. A neighborhood friend and I had already agreed to join together. My reneging on our agreement did not feel good but my price was not so high that Dad could not meet it. As events unfolded, it worked well. My friend was rejected by the military due to a broken arm in childhood that didn't mend properly. So, I would have gone alone.

The night finally came for me to leave for Tanganyika (now Tanzania) for a visit with my mother's uncle, a missionary. B.O.A.C. (British Overseas Airways Corporation) told my father they'd look after me like a mother hen. What a hollow promise. Once airborne, I was totally alone and as the lights from Houston disappeared, I was nervous. I knew the places I'd stop at, I just didn't know what to do when I got to them. While walking around Europe, I lost considerate weight. I never saw anyone eating – rather, they were all at sidewalk restaurants sipping coffee beneath large "Cinzano" signs. I was too shy to collar someone and say, "Where does someone get a bite to eat around here?" I finally discovered the restaurants were often inside, behind a bamboo curtain.

While wandering in a youth induced fog, I found a Greek guide in Athens who swore he had been the guide to Charles Ripley during one of Ripley's visits. His English was poor and I left Greece knowing little more about it than when I had arrived.

When I traveled on to land in Nairobi, Kenya, I went on the town, found some liquid courage and left extravagant tips. The following day a small plane, making shuttle stops took me to my final destination, Mbeya, Tanganyika. I got off the plane and to my shock there was no one to meet me. An older lady, a nun, asked, "Do you want to go into town?" Since the airport was tiny and virtually empty, I mumbled "yes", and we were taken to the town center. Mbeya was a fair sized trade center loaded with East Indian shop keepers and Africans selling produce. I suddenly realized I did not even have my great uncle's address. I recalled however, some letters Mom had received from him were from a place called Chimala. What could I do then but go to Chimala to seek him out? Somehow, I found my way to the police commissioner's office. He was a stately Brit helping to maintain what was still a British colony. He said, "You're in luck, there is a bus that leaves for Chimala one time a week and it leaves tomorrow morning". I thought I'd take a hotel room for the night and put myself on the bus crowded with people, cargo, and chickens. I later found out Chimala was an area possibly the size of Rhode Island. No one there spoke English and, after the sunset, hyenas, leopards, and lions came out in force as lords of the night. It was not impossible that, had I made it to Chimala alone, I might have ended up being dinner for something wild and hungry. But fate was kind. As I prepared to leave the commissioner's office, my great uncle walked in saying, "Sorry old boy, we had a flat on the way in". Do I need to say I was delighted to see him? We spent the night in a Mbeya hotel which was rather different. In the colonies, you had to wear a tie to supper if you only had a t-shirt. After dinner, the guests would have a "sundowner" (a pint of beer) and some would repair to the billiards table. I had my own room and was told to put my shoes outside the door before sleeping. The next morning your shoes would be returned, nicely polished. I awoke near dawn with a large black man standing over my bed preparing me tea.

My relatives lived atop an escarpment named Ailsa, which was only about 65 miles from Mbeya, but the trip took 4 hours. The road to the top was narrow and winding, and in later years was abandoned as too dangerous to travel and maintain. Their compound consisted of two long, rectangular houses built by the Germans before the English kicked them out in WWI. Despite the Germans being a tall people, the doors were short. And in the old European style, even in castles, to get from one room to another you had to go outside. There were no inside connecting doors. The front porch ran the length of the building and since they ran the generator for several hours each night, you could sit on the veranda and read until bedtime. Unlike so much of Africa, the escarpment was high enough to be cool. One night during that glorious summer with the seasons being reversed, we got a "southern" and jackets were put on against the cool. But usually, the weather was ideal, and there was such beauty. One road leading away from the compound was lined with trees in a European fashion, and about a mile from the compound was a cold, fast moving stream with an 8-foot waterfall. I could hike there after breakfast and stand atop rocks to dive into the base of the waterfall. The water had long before bored out the bottom making it sufficiently deep. Still, the water was unbearably cold, and the dive was immediately followed by a frantic swim to the bank. After the brief dip, I could sun myself in a high sand pit and see smoke in the distance coming from the compound as my Aunt Sadie prepared lunch. Partly for the help, partly to provide employment, they used numerous locals as tractor drivers, houseboys, and farm workers. My relatives were the only employers for many miles. They grew quite attached to the workers. One boy, just preteen and with one blind eye, introduced himself as Adonadile and asked for a job. My great uncle grew to love him as a son. The first pay Adonadile received, he spent on a blanket, not for himself, but for his family. He was the man of the house, his father having died. Today, in 2010, Adonadile is a grandfather; it is hard to picture. Gideon, our "houseboy" was actually middle-aged. He would say no one had offered him enough cows for his daughter, but we all really knew that good father did not want his daughter to leave home. I've certainly hoped they eventually worked matters out. I only know Adonadile was more of a man at 13 than I was at 21 and Gideon was twice the man I'll ever be. Shortly before I arrived, leopards had made a raid on an isolated cattle pen, killing the cattle and the woman and child watching the herd. Gideon and some of the other men went into a deep gorge armed only with spears (the British government would only allow locals a single shot gun and few could afford one) to thin out the leopards. One man speared a leopard and when he went to finish it with his panga (machete) its mate leaped on his back and clawed him to death.

I was later taken on a safari and have regretted it the rest of my life, though I was thrilled at the time. But of all animals only leopards and man seem to enjoy killing. The lion kills what he can carry away to eat. Once the blood lust is upon the leopard, he seems most reluctant to stop.

Life in the compound was the most idyllic I have known. My great uncle's partner in the work had a son my age and a daughter just old enough to carry on a flirtation. The compound was almost self-sufficient. The coffee was from their coffee plantings below, the wheat for bread from their wheat fields, the meat from their livestock, the eggs from their chickens, and the milk from their cow, Corona. Each day our beds would be made with a little piece of white chocolate placed on the pillow and other than attending church services, I had no responsibilities. I practiced spear throwing and while I began my hikes in boots with my .270, before long, I was in tennis shoes and Bermuda shorts, carrying only a spear. A finer summer could not have been had. It was clean living around wonderful people who were busy at God's work. I thought going to Africa, however, and having horns to hang on the wall would make me feel powerful. Yet after all of it, I barely had the power to blow my own nose. Power is largely an illusion. I've met Hindus who will tell you that everything we can touch, see, or smell is an illusion. And if you define illusion as something that is here briefly and then disappears, they are correct.

Upon my return from Africa, I dutifully enrolled in college, but my heart wasn't in it. If some people are late bloomers then I was a century plant. I went for 1½ years, failing two subjects largely due to skipping classes, and talked my frustrated father into allowing me to volunteer for the draft. However, by age 19, I was considerably better equipped to deal with the army. Even so, if I thought I was reasonably tough, a winter with the infantry in Ft. Carson, Colorado tenderized me. My next duty station was Ft. Bliss at El Paso. It was like paradise after the frozen hell of Carson. There in Juarez, just across the border, I found romantic love.

Soon however, we were sent to Korea as part of the occupation force. Once again the winters were terrible, but R&R to Japan gave me an experience of how grand the orient can be. There, in Tokyo, I had a brief fling with one of the Bluebells, the lido de Paris group performing at the Mikado. She had a role as attendant to Elizabeth Taylor in Cleopatra and gave me a pretty publicity photo. She wanted further contact but she was simply too sophisticated for me to feel comfortable with. When the troupe came to Las Vegas she contacted me, but I passed. I was never convinced a showgirl could settle down into a routine wife – Quien sabe?

After the army I decided college wasn't as bad as I had originally thought. I would work while going to school, save all I possibly could and leave for a summer in Europe. With practice I was becoming ever more relaxed and adroit at travel. It is as though we are born in a giant house and I don't want to see only the bedroom. I want to see the living room, attic, basement, and all adjoining rooms. I know now time won't let me. I've seen 63 countries but the U.S. recognizes over 125. But I feel no disappointment. I've seen my share and that of several others. I have regrets and sometimes the ghosts come for me in the night. That is when I like a dog in bed – something alive to touch that will not say "what do you want, I have to go to work tomorrow". Even so, travel and village work are two things I'll never regret. And so, when a friend read my manuscript, she suggested I tell more of myself, and my current life. Now I have done that. I have told all I can face in one lump. May you, the reader be haunted by fewer ghosts than me, and live long and happy.

AFTERWORD

The book you've read, despite prima facie gleanings, is not generally about being a memoir. The history it records is for the purpose of sharing what might well be encountered if the reader selects his own village and acts on that selection. It is then, roughly speaking, a How-to guide. At its most base level, it indicates the reader can move into any super poor village, speak to whatever authorities exist, ask what needs to be done, and then act on that information. As an outsider with funds, he is regarded as one who will take charge and make things happen. No one ever asks, "Who gave you permission to come here?" If they took that stand, it might be a good indicator you have selected a village that is not as poor as you thought.

At best you will make life better for hundreds for many years. At a minimum, you will spread around desperately needed money in a community that has none. Neither are bad ends and I have little patience for those who criticize legitimate bread issue charities, big or small.

I did return to Yucatan in 2008. I later found my paraplegic girl, a teenager, had been raped. But from the rape came a healthy baby boy who is very loved by the entire family.

It was gratifying to see in 2010, after Haiti's massive earthquake, how the citizenry could come together, albeit for a short time, to save their fellow countrymen. Yet in no time, Anderson Cooper was reporting on large scale looting. What conclusions can be drawn from this? Can Haitians march in lockstep to a brighter tomorrow? Heads of U. S. agencies and journalists came on television with their pronouncements of what it will take to make Haiti a success. They used formally en vogue words such as "empowerment", or "pride', "cooperation" – all good words which never put a single loaf of bread into the hands of a hungry person. These are all words that find their relevancy in a higher economic rung of the ladder. Talk, and the building of a stronger national ego, is a weak elixir for hunger.

It seems to always take days, if not weeks for assistance to arrive at the scene of such a disaster. This is understandable when one thinks of thousands of tons of foods and medical supplies. But I have always found a very quick if limited, start is advantageous. Small instantaneous supplies can make hope spring alive, and are more potent than promises, particularly in areas where television, radio, and newspapers might not be operable. In my youth, Galveston had a celebration of the early summer called "Splash Day". Thousands showed for it, and it had the result of moving congested crowds of the city, to the beach. Small planes and helicopters would fly over the ocean not far from shore and drop hundreds of corks which would float into the beach. Many of the cords had numbers on them. Those with numbers would be taken into redemption centers and traded for prizes. My dad and I, being strong swimmers, would get first look at some of the corks and one year won an automobile tire, a cake, and a man's wallet. I am not suggesting a Splash Day for disaster areas, but a small number of flights, beginning on day one, could air drop light, dried food and water packets throughout the city and surrounding area. This alone could block rumors that the people could not expect anything for some time or would be left to stew in their own juices. The man on the street always becomes quickly frustrated by having no utilities or resources, tons of aid later notwithstanding. Announcements of where the airdrops would be made could have impact on moving people from a devastated point A to a better point B. The air drops should not be in large pallets, as was finally done, as such only serve as a magnet for a clique of thugs who claim dispersal rights. Rather they should be in loose individual packets. A man with a meal and water, even for a day, is unlikely to start a "frenzy of looting", for that day at least. If you had a suitcase with 100,000 dollars in it, and dropped it intact, it is most unlikely to be widely dispersed. If you had 100,000 one dollar bills being sprayed over an area it is unlikely that any one person or small group could gather it all. It is at least as likely to find its way to a needy person as the videos I've seen of aid workers handing out single packets through the bars to outstretched hands.

It would seem to me that cremation spots could be quickly assigned (burial may be highly impractical in areas near the sea with a high water table) and a photo taken of each body prior to cremation for family identification. Likewise sign in sheets could be liberally posted so that family could check the lists to determine if their missing member lives. This would not be unlike what occurred after the Holocaust.

It was noteworthy to me, that none of the television pundits in their pedantic analysis of what Haiti needs, mentioned its lack of natural resources, the over-population problem, and the ever shrinking size of farms due to an antiquated French inheritance system. Small islands, worldwide, have problems that cannot be offset by pretty beaches, gorgeous sunsets, and an eagerness for the tourist dollar. Given the sheer number of islands, Haiti might be suited to manufacturing, or to assembly plants. Thousands of islands continue to use American size cars which are expensive to buy, maintain, and run. The solutions might be somewhere between pedicabs and the $2,500 new car of the Tata Motor Company of India. Given their extreme poverty, an every-man-for-himself attitude would prevail among any peoples of any country. The abuse of Haiti by so much of the world, for such a long time, makes even its progress to present day status seem outstanding.

www.ingramcontent.com/pod-product-compliance
Lightning Source LLC
Chambersburg PA
CBHW020435290526
45785CB00002B/864